Adolphus William Ward

# Epochs of church history

The Counter - Reformation

Adolphus William Ward

**Epochs of church history**
*The Counter - Reformation*

ISBN/EAN: 9783742842848

Manufactured in Europe, USA, Canada, Australia, Japa

Cover: Foto ©Andreas Hilbeck / pixelio.de

Manufactured and distributed by brebook publishing software (www.brebook.com)

Adolphus William Ward

**Epochs of church history**

### Epochs of Church History

EDITED BY

PROFESSOR MANDELL CREIGHTON.

THE COUNTER-REFORMATION.

# Epochs of Church History.

Edited by Professor MANDELL CREIGHTON.

Fcap. 8vo, price 2s. 6d. each.

THE ENGLISH CHURCH IN OTHER LANDS. By the Rev. H. W. TUCKER, M.A.

THE HISTORY OF THE REFORMATION IN ENGLAND. By the Rev. GEORGE G. PERRY, M.A.

THE CHURCH OF THE EARLY FATHERS. By ALFRED PLUMMER, D.D.

THE EVANGELICAL REVIVAL IN THE EIGHTEENTH CENTURY. By the Rev. J. H. OVERTON, M.A.

A HISTORY OF THE UNIVERSITY OF OXFORD. By the Hon. G. C. BRODRICK, D.C.L.

A HISTORY OF THE UNIVERSITY OF CAMBRIDGE. By J. BASS MULLINGER, M.A.

THE CHURCH AND THE ROMAN EMPIRE. By the Rev. A. CARR.

THE CHURCH AND THE PURITANS, 1570–1660. By HENRY OFFLEY WAKEMAN M.A.

THE CHURCH AND THE EASTERN EMPIRE. By the Rev. H. F. TOZER, M.A.

HILDEBRAND AND HIS TIMES. By the Rev. W. R. W. STEPHENS, M.A.

THE ENGLISH CHURCH IN THE MIDDLE AGES. By the Rev. W. HUNT, M.A., Trinity College, Oxford.

THE POPES AND THE HOHENSTAUFEN. By UGO BALZANI.

THE COUNTER-REFORMATION. By A. W. WARD, Litt. D.

*IN PREPARATION.*

THE ARIAN CONTROVERSY. By H. M. GWATKIN, M.A., Lecturer and late Fellow of St. John's College, Cambridge.

THE GERMAN REFORMATION. By Prof. MANDELL CREIGHTON, M.A., D.C.L.

WYCLIF AND THE BEGINNINGS OF THE REFORMATION. By REGINALD LANE POOLE, M.A., Balliol College, Oxford.

CHURCH AND STATE IN MODERN TIMES.

THE REFORMATION IN ENGLAND.

THE WARS OF RELIGION.

THE CHURCH AND THE TEUTONS.

CHRISTIANITY AND ISLAM.

MONKS AND FRIARS.

---

LONDON: LONGMANS, GREEN, & CO.

# THE
# COUNTER-REFORMATION.

BY

ADOLPHUS WILLIAM WARD, Litt.D.

PROFESSOR OF HISTORY IN THE OWENS COLLEGE,
VICTORIA UNIVERSITY.

LONDON:
LONGMANS, GREEN, AND CO.
1889.

# PREFACE.

It is not always easy to define the correct use of even so well-worn a phrase as 'the Counter-Reformation.' I have, however, done my best to suggest such a definition in the brief Synopsis which I have prefixed to the following Essay, and which will perhaps under the circumstances not be regarded as altogether superfluous. Of the movement known under this name, I can hardly hope in the following sketch to have indicated more than the chief aspects, avoiding, as I very sincerely trust, at all events the worst of the pitfalls in the ground traversed. Religious partisanship, deplorable as it is in elaborate narratives, would be unbearable in a mere summary.

As is well known, the characteristic powers of Ranke's genius as a historian were never exercised more conspicuously than in tracing the co-operation of religious and political purposes and motives in the period of the Catholic Reaction. Besides his *History of the Popes*, his *French History*—perhaps the most finished of all his great works—will from this point of view always remain invaluable to the student. Still, even with these works, and Baron (now Count) von Hübner's admirable monograph on Sixtus V. before me, I have found Moritz Brosch's *Geschichte des Kirchenstaates* (1880) a most useful manual of the history of Papal *government* in the sixteenth and seventeenth centuries. Of late the attempt has been made to treat the movement of the Counter-Reformation after a more concentrated fashion; but, unfortunately for me, Maurenbrecher's *Geschichte der Katholischen Reformation* (1880) has not yet advanced beyond its first volume (up to the death of Clement VII.). On the other hand, Martin Philippson's *Contre-Révolution Religieuse* (1884), which concludes with the dissolution of the Council of Trent, is complete within its limits; but my attention was not directed to this work till I was revising the first draft of my own little volume, which I hope has benefited from M. Philippson's lucid exposition. From Mr. J. A. Symonds' two volumes on *The Catholic Reaction* (which form the final portion of his *Renaissance in Italy*), I could not, though joining issue with some of his conclusions, fail to derive many valuable hints. There can be no necessity for reciting here the authorities, old and new, on such special parts of my subject as the Council of Trent, the Spanish Mystics, the Edict of Restitution, and the like. A bibliography of the history of the Counter-Reformation might indeed be a welcome gift to students, but if offered here, it would be out of place, or at least out of proportion. A. W. W.

MANCHESTER, *March* 22, 1888.

# SYNOPSIS.

A WELL-KNOWN sentence in Macaulay's Essay on Ranke's 'History of the Popes' asserts, correctly enough, that in a particular epoch of history 'the Church of Rome, having lost a large part of Europe, not only ceased to lose, but actually regained nearly half of what she had lost.' Any fairly correct use of the familiar phrase 'the Counter-Reformation' must imply that this remarkable result was due to a movement pursuing two objects, originally distinct, though afterwards largely blended, viz., the regeneration of the Church of Rome, and the recovery of the losses inflicted upon her by the early successes of Protestantism.

*The Counter-Reformation defined.*

If, then, the twofold purpose of the movement in question be kept in view, there can be no difficulty in deciding what ought, and what ought not, to be included within the limits of the present sketch. Outside them must be left the schemes, projected or essayed, for altering the doctrine or amending the practice of the Church of Rome which preceded the first appearance of Luther as her assailant in principle. Neither, on the other hand, ought we to occupy ourselves here with the resistance offered by the Establishment to its opponents before the time when with this resistance was coupled the design of self-reformation,—of reformation, as it has been usually styled, 'from within.' The short pontificate of Adrian VI. was animated by an eager desire to combine both ends; but inasmuch as its aspirations remained altogether unaccomplished, no place belongs to it in the body of my narrative. The earliest continuous endeavour to regenerate the Church of Rome without impairing her cohesion dates from the Papacy of Paul III. within which also falls the outbreak of the first religious war of the century. Thus the two impulses which it was the special task of the Counter-Reformation to fuse were brought into immediate contact. The onset of the combat is marked by the formal establishment of the Jesuit Order as a militant agency devoted alike to both the purposes of the Counter-Reformation, and by the meeting of the Council of Trent under conditions excluding from its programme the task of conciliation. Of the restoration of the Roman supremacy in England, which occurred soon afterwards, a brief notice will in the present connexion suffice, since this proceeding, accidental in itself, was soon rendered futile by another turn of the wheel. It was in the final sittings of the Council of Trent that the Jesuits first victoriously

*Preliminary effort.*

*Beginning of the Counter-Reformation as a continuous movement.*

*Height of the movement.*

asserted a control over the policy of the Church of Rome; and the promulgation of the Conciliar Decrees, while introducing into the life of that Church a series of enduringly beneficent changes, at the same time formed the first systematic attempt to obstruct the progress of Protestantism 'along the whole line.' The date of this promulgation, therefore, announces the opening of the period in which the Counter-Reformation put forth its full force.

*The weakness of divided Protestantism.*

At no previous time had the movement been so well supported by the tendency on the Protestant side to harden and perpetuate internal differences of doctrine, and thus to break up the front presented to the common foe. The period during which the Counter-Reformation continuously displays a most extraordinary and versatile energy closes with the collapse of the deliberate attempt of Philip of Spain, as the indefatigable champion, but not the henchman, of Rome, to master the destinies of Western Christendom. The last ten years of his life reached from the dissipation of the Spanish Armada, an expedition designed to avenge many martyrdoms *in partibus*, to the pacification which enabled Henry IV. of France to sign the Edict of Nantes. During the years which followed, the sense of the imminent renewal of the conflict lay heavy upon Europe, and the agents of the Counter-Reformation had to content themselves with undermining defences which it would have been inopportune to seek to take by storm. And thus their side was the

*Decline of the movement.*

better prepared when the struggle in which they were unceasingly engaged merged in the Great War—in parts of its course only a religious war—of the seventeenth century. Though in the earlier part of the contest the cause of Rome was completely victorious, so that it seemed feasible to satisfy the claims of the Reaction by imperial edict, the balance was in some measure redressed by later events. Inasmuch, however, as the movement for the reconquest of what Rome had lost had ceased to aim, except incidentally, at the reform of the Church, it can hardly be said to have been any longer the Counter-Reformation proper which was ruled out of date by the Peace of Westphalia. The twofold movement which this Essay has in view did not wholly come to an end, but it lost its combined historical significance among the complications of the Thirty Years' War.

*The Counter-Reformation merged in the Thirty Years' War.*

# CONTENTS.

## CHAPTER I.

INTRODUCTORY . . . . . . . . . 1

## CHAPTER II.

THE BEGINNINGS OF THE CATHOLIC REVIVAL . 07

## CHAPTER III.

THE COUNCIL OF TRENT . . . . . . . 58

## CHAPTER IV.

THE COUNTER-REFORMATION AT ITS HEIGHT . . . 101

## CHAPTER V

THE RELIGIOUS CONFLICT MERGED IN THE GREAT WAR . 152

INDEX . . . . . . . . . . . 197

# THE COUNTER-REFORMATION.

## CHAPTER I.

### *INTRODUCTORY.*

In the history of the Western Church, while united under the acknowledged supremacy of the Bishop of Rome, there have been but few periods in which its administration and the life of its clergy have been exempt from censure. During the latter half of the Middle Ages the *reformation* of these constant objects of complaint was aimed at in a long succession of efforts. Fresh bitterness was added to these grievances, and the condition of the Papacy itself took the most prominent place among them, when, on the first decline of the Papal authority under Boniface VIII., there followed the abasement of Avignon and the ignominy of the Schism. Yet, at the same time, a belief sprang up that the end of these scandalous divisions would also be the end of the existing degeneracy. During the period of the Œcumenical Councils which ensued, the task of reforming the Church in both head and members

*Earlier attempts at reformation in the Church of Rome, before the Conciliar period.*

*In the Conciliar period.*

appeared at last to have been undertaken by the Church herself, to the decrees of whose representative assemblies the Pope himself was called upon to submit. But the Council of Pisa was dissolved by its own nominee, Alexander V. At Constance, had the majority persevered, it would have redressed nearly all the grievances urged against the Church within the century preceding Luther's first assault. But the success of any comprehensive measure of reform became impossible after the German nation's demand that the question of general reformation should precede the choice of a new Pope had been defeated by the election of Martin V. The revived activity of the old papal system was made manifest by the results of the Council of Basel. Of some of its earlier decrees France secured the substantial benefit to her own Church in the Pragmatic Sanction of Bourges, but the Empire was skilfully deprived of them in the Concordate of Vienna. On the main issue as to supremacy, the Papal authority in the end prevailed over the Conciliar.

After the Council which burnt Hus and the Council which transacted with the Hussites had alike sought to take the work of administration and disciplinary reform out of the hands of the Popes, they, in their turn, during the next period, so far as possible ignored the decrees of both assemblies. Whatever promises were made by Nicolas V. and his successors down to Alexander VI., they took care not to repeat the Conciliar experiment. Thus to the Papacy itself was now left the initiative of Church reform; nor

*Between the close of the Conciliar period and the beginning of the Protestant reformation.*

was the need of it ignored by all these pontiffs. Nicolas V. sent Cardinal Cusanus (Nicolas of Cues) to reform the German monasteries. Paul II. before his election promised a thorough reform of both Curia and clergy. And even at the close of this period Alexander VI. was at no loss for appropriate replies to the representations on the subject addressed to him from Spain. In truth, however, nothing short of heroic energy inspired by apostolic zeal could have made reformers of Popes breathing the intellectual and moral atmosphere of the later Italian Renascence. The difficulties pressing upon these pontiffs as Italian princes led them to regard themselves essentially as such, without at the same time losing sight of the influence inseparable from their religious attributes. Under Sixtus IV. and Innocent VIII., simony and nepotism were the right and the left arm of the Papal government, absorbed in the struggle for territorial acquisitions. Alexander VI. and his bastard stood face to face with the idea of transforming the temporal power into a hereditary dominion, while at the same time the spiritual envelope of the Papacy had become transparent like a Coan vesture. Julius II. put a stop to a condition of things which even Renascence consciences could no longer bear, although he was more distinctively than any of his predecessors an Italian prince, patriot, and politician; but his summoning of the Lateran Council (1512) was merely an act of self-defence against the use made by his political enemies of the growing cry for ecclesiastical reformation.

*The initiation of reformation left to the Popes.*

For, notwithstanding the apathy or passive resistance of the Popes, the nations of the West had not yet learned to despair of a reformation of the Church by her own constituted authorities. Nowhere was a more practical shape assumed by these cravings than in Spain, the country destined afterwards to become the chief source of the counter-reformation. The movement for the regeneration of the Spanish Church under Ferdinand and Isabella, of which Ximenez was the directing spirit, was in its political objects based on the Concordate of 1482, and it had a considerable intellectual affinity with the Renascence. Yet, notwithstanding these vital differences, it had much in common with the Counter-Reformation itself, besides the co-operation of the Inquisition, revived in Spain under a new constitution (1483). Thus it was a Spaniard, Carvajal, who thought to crown his demonstrations on behalf of Church reform when, in company with four other cardinals, members of the Sacred College, he summoned a council to Pisa in despite of the Pope (1511). At first it seemed as if this daring stroke would be attended with success. A few meetings were held at Pisa and at Milan under the ægis of Louis XII. of France, whose national policy was consistently directed to the restoration of the Pragmatic Sanction, nominally abolished by Louis XI. The summons to Pisa at first likewise received the sanction of the Emperor Maximilian I.; for the widespread desire in Germany for reformation had found frequent expression at the Diets of the Empire. The *gravamina* presented at Worms in 1510 are in fact largely identical with the complaints which the Councils of Constance and Basel had

*General desire for reformation.*

*Spain.*

*Pressure put upon the Papacy.*

in vain sought to redress, and for which there seemed no enduring remedy left except the placing of the German Church under independent national control. But the absence, notwithstanding recent changes, of any real national unity, and the characteristic collapse of Maximilian's zeal for Church reform, wrecked all these aspirations and endeavours; and in the end the Emperor and the princes, although unrepresented at the Lateran Council, solemnly acknowledged it. The same futile course was taken by Spain and by England.

While the Lateran Council was still in progress, and just after the War of the Holy League had driven the French from Italy, Julius II. died, and was succeeded by Leo X. (March 1513). The drastic measures taken by the new Pope at the beginning of his reign prepared a virtually complete victory for the Papal policy. The chief of the reforming cardinals submitted; Francis I., though in the flush of victory, accepted a Concordate (1515) as a compromise of the French national demands; and the Lateran Council before its close (December 1516) confirmed the bull *Unam Sanctam*, which declared it 'necessary to salvation for every human being to be subject to the authority of the Pope.' The question of reformation, on the other hand, though by no means ignored, was not materially advanced by this merely Italian assembly; the Papal abuses proper were virtually passed by; and when, before separating, the Council sanctioned the levy of contributions for a crusade, both the Spanish clergy and the Estates of the Empire suspected a Florentine trick.

The Fifth Lateran Council had made it clear that

all hope of a reformation of the Church from within must be abandoned. Except where the practice of the Papal policy was restricted by concordates, princes, prelates, and peoples suffered in common from the impositions of Rome, and no class of society could be blind to the results of the progressive decay of both efficiency and morality among the clergy. More especially was this degeneracy to be deplored in the case of the monastic orders, so many of which had been established with the avowed purpose of reanimating and reinvigorating popular religion. Princes and prelates were in addition as jealous as they had always been of Papal claims which impaired their own sovereign or episcopal authority. Surrounded by a new splendour since the subjection of the New World to its supremacy, the Papacy had at home outwitted its adversaries, and could afford to contemn its censors. What remedy remained?

*A Papal reformation no longer hoped for.*

To this question two different answers were proposed by two great men; but by preferring Luther's, the opponents of the Papal system of Church government made the answer of Erasmus impossible. Accordingly, the experiment was left untried whether Western Christendom might be *educated* into seeking and securing for itself a purer Church, with a more reasonable presentment of religion. The actual mould was soon burst by the fiery metal impulsively poured into it. Rome spoke in the matter of the Lutheran heresy (June 1520), at the very time when, in his fulminant address to the Christian nobles of Germany, Luther was detailing his own ideas of indispensable Church reform—ideas far more moderate than the

*Luther and the Papacy.*

language in which they were clothed. Eleven months later, he was, with the help of a discreditable manœuvre, formally placed under the ban of the Empire. But the edict was far from generally executed in the Empire, and a prospect still existed of closing the breach made by Luther's well-timed boldness, when the pontificate of Leo X. suddenly came to an end (December 1521).

The elevation to the Papal chair of Adrian VI., the Emperor's late tutor and actual regent in Spain, may Papacy of Adrian VI. have been primarily due to the fact that he was an absentee from the conclave where *all* the cardinals present desired their own election. But of course he was a peculiarly safe choice in the eyes of the imperial party and of its accepted nominee, Cardinal Giulio de Medici, when the election of the latter proved impossible; while, as a distinguished scholastic theologian, he seemed worthier of trust than perhaps a prominent reformer or two among the candidates. In his antecedents there was nothing to alarm conservative instincts. When an academical celebrity at Louvain, though all but an ascetic in habits of life and most open-handed in his charities, he had been a very notable pluralist. The doctrine of Papal infallibility, which his learned pen had in those days taken upon itself to confute, was one which the Church had still left undefined. As regent in Spain, while his resignation, on his appointment to the see of Tortosa, of some of his other preferments might seem the act of a purist, he had shown great activity in the office of Inquisitor-General (which he retained till within a few days of his death). On the announcement of his election to the Papacy, Adrian submitted to this crowning manifestation of the Divine will with a solemn sense of the dignity of the office to which he was called, and in which it seemed impossible for him to look upon himself as the creature of the Emperor. The circumstances of his election were at the time, as afterwards, much misrepresented; but how could he have failed from the first to appreciate its significance, and to recall the times when another Charles had, under the Papacy of another Adrian, fought the battles of the Holy See against its foes? Nor when the general character of the ecclesiastical policy of Charles V. is considered, together with the nature of his personal relations to Adrian VI., can it be denied that the union of these two potentates seemed to offer a unique chance of a Catholic counter-reformation, *i.e.*, a regeneration of the Church combined with the extirpation of heresy.

But Charles V. could not take either of these objects in hand, any more than set about his desired crusade against the Turks, till he had carried to a successful issue his war with France, in which he not unnaturally thought himself entitled to the support of the new Pope. Adrian, on the other hand, though longing for the restoration of peace between the Christian powers, in order that they might in common make war upon the encroaching infidel, would fain have brought about this peace as mediator rather than as the ally of one of the combatants. In the end—just before his death—he had to fall in with the Emperor's proposals (August 1523); but during nearly the whole of his short Papacy there had been little real cordiality between the pair, and the reformation of the Church was hardly if at all mentioned in their correspondence. Thus it was without the aid of his imperial pupil that Pope Adrian VI. addressed himself to the task imposed upon him by his lofty conception of his office. At Rome, his election, as that of a foreigner, had been received with the most open manifestations of ill-will; he neither possessed, nor would he have condescended to use, the arts by which disaffection might have been appeased; he seems not even to have been master of the Italian tongue. At first he may have derived some encouragement from the speech by which Cardinal Carvajal welcomed him in the name of the Sacred College. The seven *recordationes* presented to him dwelt on the grievous corruptions in the Church, but contained no allusion to the religious movement in Germany, of which it was still the fashion at Rome to make light. Even more significant was the elaborate memorial drawn up by Ægidius of Viterbo, General of the Order of St. Augustine, and submitted to the Pope by the reforming party among the cardinals. This document appeals to the Pope, in whose election the hand of God is manifest, to restore the Church, beginning with an enquiry into the fallen condition of the Papacy itself, as the real source of the widespread ecclesiastical corruption. The power of the keys ought to be reduced to the limits of ancient usage, and any abuse of it scrupulously avoided. Pluralities and *compositions* should be wholly abolished; *reservations* confined to exceptional cases, and *commends* kept within due measure.

The entire judicial administration of the Church should be revised, the supreme court at Rome (*rota*) re-organised, the chamber of finance (*camera*) reformed, and a commission appointed to enquire into the new offices by which Leo X. had so largely increased his expenditure and his debts. As for the life and morals of the clergy at large, it would be desirable to carry out the decrees of the Lateran Council. On the other side, while the memorial insisted on the necessity of restricting improper concessions granted in concordates to temporal princes, it demanded the rigorous execution of the Edict of Worms against the new German heresy. The Holy See should hasten to take advantage of the readiness of Bohemia to be reconciled to it; while, with a view no doubt to the suppression of the more recent and more dangerous religious revolt, it should use its best endeavours to mediate peace between the Empire, France, and England. The entire memorial might have served as a text-book for the actual Counter-Reformation.

Coming from Spain, Adrian VI. must have received these demands and recommendations, all of which were completely in harmony with both his experiences and his opinions, as a challenge to his conscience. The plague was raging at Rome, and he was himself enfeebled by illness; but he resolved to remain in the city. On the very day after his coronation (September 1, 1522), he annulled all steps taken by the Sacred College since his election for the filling up of benefices; and soon afterwards (October 11th) he published the Chancery rules, which he had first put forth in Spain (April

*His attempt at a counter-reformation.*

24th), and which revoked all reservations made, or expectancies granted, in his name. He soon showed his intention to respond to nearly all the demands of the reforming cardinals, by declaring against pluralities, renouncing the right of ordering reservations, and seeking to limit the operation, and thereby to diminish the issue, of indulgences. But the best proof of his resolve to 'oust Simon Magus from his time-honoured seat' is to be found in his strenuous declaration against abuses which at Rome had come to be considered institutions. He reduced his household in a spirit of primitive simplicity, and adapted his military establishment to the model of Sparta on a peace footing. He tried to prevent his subjects from bearing arms, and the cardinals from granting sanctuary. And while he announced his intention of abolishing the multitudinous new offices created by his predecessor, he incurred by his cold and almost precisian reserve the contemptuous hatred of the Roman artistic and literary world.

If Adrian VI. actually supposed that his well-meant but crude efforts would be crowned with success, he had reckoned without Rome. The population of the city desired money to be spent in, among, and upon it. The official world of the Curia opposed with deadly determination this sudden deviation of the Papacy into the path of administrative reform. Adrian was laughed at as a Platonic idealist among the Romulean rabble; he was execrated for appointing Flemings and Germans to some of the most confidential of the offices left in his court; not a grain of popular sympathy was from first to last bestowed upon his endeavours. But the resistance to these of course centred in the College of Cardinals, to which, with the exception of one nomination immediately before his death, he made no additions. His policy was indeed here supported by Caraffa, who, like Adrian, had imbibed ideas of ecclesiastical reform in Spain, and by one or two others. But even Cajetano (de Vio), who had learnt patience from the results of the Lateran Council, advised deliberation, and Soderini uttered warnings fraught with the experience of three pontificates. Thus the Pope was left to carry on the struggle nearly alone; nor is it wonderful that he should have had resort to men of piety and learning, on whose sympathy he thought himself able to count, and among them to his countryman Erasmus, the foremost man of letters of the age. The correspondence between Adrian VI. and Erasmus, however, shows that, whatever may have been at this time the great scholar's mental attitude towards the Lutheran reformation, he had scant sympathy to spare for the counter-movement as conceived by the actual head of the Church. He declined the Pope's invitation to Rome, taking occasion to express both his annoyance at being charged there with the authorship of the new heresy, and his conviction that no advice of his was called for if that heresy was to be suppressed by persecution. And he was right; since, transparently honest as Pope Adrian was, he could hardly have acted in concert with an ally who invoked the sweet name of Liberty. Before the final reply of Erasmus was indited, the Pope had already entered upon the second part of his scheme of counter-reformation. Luther's patron, Frederick the Wise of Saxony, was admonished to repentance in a Papal missive, containing an attack upon Luther himself as virulent as it was ill-founded. Then, in December 1523, through his legate, Chieregati, at the Diet of Nürnberg, the Pope denounced the Lutheran movement to the Estates in the most unmeasured terms, and declared his determination to resist it. In the same breath, however, he professed his desire, but for which he would never have taken upon himself the burden of the Papacy, to reform the deformed Catholic Church. With true greatness of soul, he caused the condition of that Church to be described to the Diet as corrupt from the head downwards. The Diet replied in a very cool tone, recurring to the grievances of the German nation against the Roman Curia, and suggesting that they should be remedied *before* the proposed steps were taken against Luther. In no other way could a *modus vivendi* be found up to the meeting of a General Council, which it was hoped would soon be summoned to some suitable German city. No desire was indicated to break with the Pope, but the sanction of the Diet to the execution of the Edict of Worms was distinctly refused, and even a request on the part of the Pope for the institution of proceedings against certain preachers of heresy in Nürnberg itself was declined. The result must have been a bitter disappointment to Adrian, although in truth his difficulties at Rome left him no time for proceeding effectively against the German reformation. In the midst of them he died (September 14, 1523). At his death-bed, the cardinals to whom he commended the cause of the Church are said to have responded with eager enquiries as to the disposal of his personal pro-

<small>His failure and death.</small>

perty. His great endeavour was doomed to failure, if only because he ignored the most obvious considerations of policy, and sought to accomplish his ends forthwith and unassisted, save by the sanctity of his office. Sacred no doubt it still was to many minds, but hardly to those of all the cardinals, not to speak of the protonotaries, referendaries, solicitors, writers of the archives, *collectores plumbi*, and other officials at Rome. Adrian expected, with a confidence either childish or sublime, that everything, including the Emperor's necessities, would bend to the demands of his own zeal. He brought no other leverage to bear upon the twofold task which he had set himself to accomplish, and Christendom might indeed have cried miracle had he lifted the load.

Adrian's successor, Clement VII. (1523–34), though not indifferent to the efforts which, in the course of his reign, religious enthusiasm continued to make at Rome, returned to the ordinary Papal methods of government and policy.

<small>The crisis of the temporal power under Clement VII.</small>

At first, indeed, he displayed some diplomatic activity on behalf of the suppression of heresy in the Empire, and put forth a thin decree bearing upon the removal of certain internal abuses. In 1524 his legate Campeggi at Ratisbon published a mandate conceived in the spirit of Adrian's reforms, and modelled on their Spanish precedents. It appears to have exercised a salutary effect upon the South German clergy, and to have approved itself to the great English Cardinal Wolsey, himself a reformer of the moderate type. The time of its publication was opportune, for a reaction against Luther's no-compromise seemed to have set in even in Germany, and a great opportunity seemed to offer itself to Erasmus and the Erasmians. But all too soon the sky was darkened by events which constitute an epoch in the history of the Papacy. Not so much by his own fault, as by that of the policy inherited by him from previous holders of the temporal power, Clement VII. had to throw himself into the arms of France and to quarrel with the Emperor. Not only did the Edict of Worms now become a dead letter, but soon the imperial army was marching upon Rome. In the *sacco di Roma* (1527) Spanish soldiers shared with German *landsknechte;* nor was it to the Protestant world alone that the judgment of Heaven seemed to have descended on the city of the Popes. Charles V., who now held Pope Clement as a prisoner in his power, might perhaps have solved the twofold question of the reformation of the Church and of the suppression of the religious revolt by simply abolishing the temporal power. Or he might have refused to restore it unless after a thorough reform of the Roman Curia and of the whole system of Papal administration, such as was actually demanded by his Spaniards. At the very least he might have carried out the plan, which he had cherished during the last three years, of assembling a General Council, whose reformatory decrees no Papal intrigues could have hindered, manipulated, or stultified. Charles V. contented himself with trusting to the weakness of the restored Pope. The demand for a Council was evaded at Bologna (November 1529), where, about the very time when Protestantism was seeking to establish itself on definite dogmatic bases, the Papacy returned to political manœuvres. Successfully resisting the Emperor's reiterated demands for a Council, Clement called in the aid of the infidel and heterodox world to redress the balance of the faithful. Thus he contrived to maintain his own political influence, and to assure the future of the house of Medici. He was warned by the Venetian Contarini that the welfare of the Church, for which it was the Pope's duty to labour, did not rest on her temporal power. The personally respectable but common-place character of Clement VII. enabled him to pass unchanged through an experience more awful than had befallen any of his predecessors. But just as the Rome of the Renascence was never again to rise from her ruins, so the Church of which Rome remained the centre was already before his death (September 1534) awake to the fact that in the epoch now at hand she could no longer remain standing in the old ways.

## CHAPTER II.

### THE BEGINNINGS OF THE CATHOLIC REVIVAL.

PAUL III. (Alexander Farnese, 1534–49) was qualified neither by his antecedents nor by his character for the task of reforming the Church, but forty years of license during his cardinalate had not altogether blunted his perception of what he might help to effect as a Pope. Very soon after his election he gave proof of his insight both into the spiritual needs of the Church and into the shortcomings of his predecessors. But unfortunately none of his responsibilities, besides the duty of upholding the temporal power, seemed to him so obvious and so pressing as the traditional Papal obligation of providing for his family. Thus he succeeded in obtaining for his descendants a respectable place as Dukes of Parma and Piacenza among the sovereign families of Italy and Europe. The really determining force of his versatile foreign policy was not religious bigotry, from which he was personally free, nor even his sincere desire for peace between the great contending powers. It was, in a word, dynastic ambition, which was, paradoxically enough, on occasion stronger in him even than the ties of blood. Not even his hatred of the ascendancy of Charles V., established by the issue of the Smalcaldic war, nor the suspicion probably entertained by him that the imperial policy was privy to the assassination of his own son (September 1547), prevented him from seeking in Charles V. a support which the dynasty of the Farnese could not spare. In the religious policy of a Pope actuated by such a master-motive it would be futile to seek for any inner consistency. The mind of Paul III., though enlightened and in some sense unprejudiced, was not moved by spiritual zeal; and thus the religious history of his reign is full of startling contrasts.

The earliest attempts in this period to regenerate the Church of Rome without breaking the mould of her existing forms are not associated with any opposition, conscious or unconscious, to the labours and aspirations of Luther and the reformers who followed in his path. In Italy, the first manifestations during the sixteenth century of a desire for a spiritual revival in the Church represent a natural reaction against the prevailing fashion of unbelief. At the Lateran Council in 1513 Leo X. had to assert by a 'constitution' the doctrine of the individual immortality of the soul. Yet neither the circle in which Leo had himself grown up, nor that which dominated Roman society under his rule, could lay claim to orthodoxy. Though Lorenzo the Magnificent and his Academy had never defied the teachings of the Church, yet their own point of view was essentially mystic and undogmatic. Leo X.'s personal interest in divinity has probably been underrated; but even in the case of a

*Spiritual movements in Italy.*

Pope it is permissible to deduce his inclinations from the company which he keeps. Thus certain pious and reflecting minds began to fear lest the most spiritual elements in the work of the Church and of her priesthood might either meet with disregard and derision, or come to be dissociated from the distinctive doctrines and practices of the Catholic religion. At some time in the course of this pontificate (1513-22) an Oratory The Oratory of Divine Love. of Divine Love was founded in the church of Sts. Sylvester and Dorothea in Trastevere at Rome, and its services and exercises were attended by a congregation of between fifty and sixty members, including the future Cardinals Contarini, Sadoleti, Ghiberti, and Caraffa. The precedent of this foundation was speedily imitated at Vicenza and in several other towns; and in the reign of Adrian VI. the movement of the Oratorians naturally threw out further fibres. Under Clement VII. the dire catastrophe which befell the city of Rome together with the Pope deprived the Renascence in Italy of its very centre and focus; nor did Rome for a long time, or the Italian Renascence ever, recover from the shock. Thus an influence in the main antagonistic to a restoration of the spiritual life and energy of the Church was permanently impaired. But for the moment this effect could not be measured; and after the sack of Rome the representatives of the Renascence and those of the religious revival were alike fugitives from its walls. Not a few of both the one and the other group found their way to Venice, a city whose own power was already on the wane, but which alone among the communities of Northern and Central Italy had remained untouched by war or foreign invasion. Theological opinion enjoyed much freedom of utterance here, and the intimate mercantile relations with Germany had given rise to a very warm interest in the new Lutheran doctrines. At Venice, then, and in the neighbouring University of Padua, there met several scholars and ecclesiastics belonging to the school of thought associated with the Oratory of Divine Love beyond the Tiber. Hither came, at least in passing, Gian Pietro Caraffa, bishop of Chieti and archbishop of Brindisi. Born of an illustrious and influential Campanian family, and trained in the best learning of the Renascence, he had been early introduced to the Papal court, and had earned distinction as nuncio at the courts of Ferdinand and Henry VIII. In Spain he had been fired by the spectacle of a genuine religious revival. Leo X. had afterwards availed himself of his theological acumen when the Lutheran heresy underwent examination; and he had been consulted on the schemes which lay so near to the heart of Adrian VI. Under Clement VII. Caraffa had withdrawn from court into a convent, though the Pope had proposed to confer upon him an extraordinary disciplinary authority over the clergy resident at Rome (May 1524); but even during the dark days in question he refused to despair of the future of the Church.

<small>Caraffa.</small>

Gasparo Contarini was a Venetian born, and an eminent senator of the republic, which he had also served on foreign missions. To whatever degree his views of the cardinal doctrine of justification may have approached Luther's, his doctrinal opinions seem to have been as broad as his conceptions of ecclesiastical government; while his conciliatory

<small>Contarini.</small>

wisdom and lofty independence of spirit were alike indigenous to the city of his origin. Other noble Venetians sympathised in the highest aspirations of the scholars of Padua, but none more ardently than

Pole.

the 'nobleman of England,' whose royal blood and generous bearing had marked him out even when a mere student in the venerable university. He probably thought himself but a sojourner in these seats of learning and culture, when in 1534 he was ordered by his royal kinsman, Henry VIII., to renounce the supremacy of the Pope. After the king had acknowledged the receipt of Pole's defence of the unity of the Church by an invitation to England, and that invitation had been declined, there could be no peace between them. But the early intercourse between Contarini and Pole, who together with Caraffa may be said to represent the opening stage of the Counter-Reformation, was animated by no purely or essentially controversial purpose. On the contrary, as Ranke has shown, the teaching of Contarini and his school, more especially on the crucial question of justification, was in actual touch with theological ideas which at this time had penetrated into various spheres of Italian society, and in their turn had much in common with Protestant doctrines proper. Least of all could these relations remain obscure at a time when the influence of the Reformation itself, besides reaching Venice from Germany, had from France and Navarre penetrated into Northern Italy, and had thence by way of Ferrara, where Calvin at one time took refuge, reached the Romagna and the immediate neighbourhood of Rome. It thus becomes easy to understand on the one hand the readiness of Contarini and his friends to entertain schemes of reunion, and on the other the determination of the Jesuits to eradicate the effects, visible in almost every city from Naples to Milan, of the insinuating literary arguments of Juan Valdez and his disciples, and of the powerful sermons of Bernardino Ochino.

Very soon after his accession in 1534, Paul III., beginning, more wisely than Adrian VI., with men instead of measures, created six new cardinals, chosen without their own knowledge, and purely on account of their religious views and sentiments. Contarini is said to have been the first nominated, and to have proposed the rest. They included, besides Caraffa and Pole, Matteo Ghiberti, the exemplary bishop of Verona, whom Leo X. had honoured, and whom 'Vida sung;' Federigo Fregoso, archbishop of Salerno, and Jacopo Sadoleti, bishop of Carpentras in France, both of whom had, like Ghiberti, frequented the Oratory of Divine Love. Sadoleti, admired far and near as a type of the elegant culture of the later Renascence, was the author of a work in which he argued that the caducity of the Church could only be cured by the introduction of a new and more vigorous discipline. Yet it was in no truculent spirit that he or those associated with him accepted the Papal nomination. When announcing his appointment to Melanchthon, and asking for the friendship of the German reformer, he declared himself not to be " the kind of man in whom difference of opinion at once gives rise to hatred."

*[marginal note: New cardinals created by Paul III.]*

The next step of Paul III. was to appoint a commission consisting of these new cardinals, together with two other members of the Sacred College, Cortese and Aleander, both of them eminent for learning, while the latter had gained reputation as a diplomatist by his exertions in Germany in connection with the bull of excommunication against Luther and the Edict of Worms. This commission was charged with the preparation of proposals, in harmony of course with accepted doctrines and traditions, for the reform of the Church. Its report is the celebrated *consilium de emendandâ ecclesiâ*. Contarini, the soul of the entire transaction, appears to have abandoned his original intention of demanding the opinion of all his colleagues on each head of the commission, but there was no lack of earnestness, or even of boldness, in their joint conclusions. The report insisted with pitiless logic upon the principle that no payment could be accepted by the Pope for any spiritual grace without the guilt of simony being incurred by him, and reflected severely on the condition of the regular orders, urging that, if they were not altogether abolished, they should at least be prohibited from receiving any more novices, while those already under their care should be dismissed. It also took occasion to reprehend the spread of irreligious teaching from academical chairs, and even from church pulpits. The influence of Contarini, who supplemented the report by tractates of his own, chiefly directed against curialistic abuses, brought about the appointment of special commissions for the execution of reforms in various branches of the Papal administration, and the issue of bulls indited in the

*Commission on Church reform.*

same spirit. The publication of the entire report was, however, postponed until it could be laid before a General Council; but to the convocation of such a council the action of the Pope seemed logically to point.

Both within and beyond the frontiers of the Empire, in Würtemberg and at Augsburg, in Saxony and in Brandenburg, in Livonia and in the Scandinavian north, as well as in England and in Switzerland, the course of events during the fourteen years which intervened between the Religious Peace of Nürnberg (1532) and the outbreak of the Smalcaldic War (1546) seemed to justify the confidence of the Protestants. In the midst of these advances of heresy, Charles V., though steadily adhering to the plan of a General Council, was involved in arduous conflicts which made it necessary for him to conciliate the Protestant interest in the Empire. In both the French wars of this period (1536-38 and 1542-44) the Sultan was the ally of Francis I.; the floodgates of Hungary stood open, and Austria and the Empire were in constant peril. The Association of Catholic Princes, formed in opposition to the League of Smalcald (1538), was under these circumstances wholly ineffective; and by the advice of Granvelle the Emperor encouraged a series of theological conferences between Roman Catholic and Lutheran divines with a view to finding a basis for re-union. Already at Frankfort (1539) the Protestants made plain their desire for a definitive settlement, and refused to hear of the intervention of a Papal nuncio in future discussions of the subject. The conferences that followed were looked forward to with many pious hopes,

*Progress of Protestantism, 1532-47.*

*Conferences on religious re-union.*

and many minds devoutly attached to the Church once more renewed their aspirations for her reformation from within. But the desired result remained unaccomplished either at Hagenau and Worms (1540), or by the more elaborate efforts made on the occasion of the Diet of Ratisbon (1541). Here failure was ensured by the efforts of French seconded by English diplomacy, and still more by the stiff-neckedness of some of the Protestant princes, led by the Elector John Frederick of Saxony, and encouraged by Luther himself. But Contarini too, who, sped by the good wishes of Pole, appeared as Papal legate, arrived at the limit of the concessions for which he was prepared on the subject of the Eucharist; and it is open to grave doubt whether his previous concessions on other points would have been ratified by the Pope. Ultimately, after the Ratisbon Interim had postponed a settlement (1541), it was decided not to submit to a future General Council even those points on which an agreement had been reached; and the failure of the entire transaction was made patent by the Emperor's renewal of the Nürnberg league of Catholic princes, of which, at his instigation, the Pope, disappointed or disillusioned, now became a member. The schism thus seemed remediless, and in the Empire the Protestant interest continued in the ascendant. Meanwhile, in Italy, under influences which had at first co-operated with the endeavours of the school or party to which Contarini and Pole belonged, a movement was already on foot which was speedily to urge the Church of Rome in a contrary direction to that of comprehension or tolerance. The pontificate of Paul

III. may (of course without exact chronological accuracy) be regarded as the birth-time of the militant orders of the Catholic reaction.

*New Orders.* The reformation of the monastic orders, recognised as necessary at Constance and actually taken in hand at Basel, had made some progress even in countries still in communion with Rome; and wherever an attempt to enforce it was made by Church or State, academical, literary, and general public opinion were, as a rule, ready with their support. Still, a wholly new impulse was given to the movement in the period now under discussion. The last order founded before the age of the Protestant reformation had been that of the *Minims*, established by Francis of Paula (canonised 1519) in Calabria, and confirmed by Sixtus IV. in 1473. The earliest monastic institution which it is possible to connect with the Catholic reaction is the organisation in 1522 by the Venetian Paolo Giustiniani at Masaccio in the Papal States of a reformed congregation of the Camaldolites, themselves an aftergrowth of the Benedictines. The reformed rule, framed by both Adrian VI. and Clement VII., was ultimately established with great rigour at Monte Corona; but inasmuch as, in accordance with the original design of the order, its operation was essentially isolating, the congregation, which spread in Italy, Germany, and Poland, could not exercise much direct influence upon the revival of religious life and sentiment. Far different was the effect of the reformation—one among many—in the great Franciscan order which Matteo de Bassi began in 1525, and which in 1528 resulted in the

*The Capuchins.*

establishment near Camerino, with the approval of Pope Clement VII., of the so-called *Capuchins*. They do not appear to have obtained full independence as an order till nearly a century later (1619), but in the meantime they had done more than enough to justify their existence. In Italy, where they began by exhibiting a self-sacrificing devotion during the ravages of the plague, they contributed more than perhaps any other agency to sustain the fidelity of the people at large to the Established Church. Though both in earlier and in later times there were among them many men of learning, including their vicar-general the celebrated Bernardino Ochino, whose apostasy could hardly have failed to damage a less robust body, it was their popular fibre which gave them their peculiar vitality. Like the Franciscans of the thirteenth and fourteenth centuries, they were the preachers of the people, and their oratory exercised its influence over a great part of Europe, often no doubt flying in the face of all canons of refinement. Thus it was not only in matters of State policy that the Capuchins were afterwards at issue with their contemporaries the Jesuits. With much of the strength of the great mendicant order of which the Capuchins were an offshoot, they combined one of the chief symptoms of its age of decay. Prohibited from depending upon any provision of their own, they resorted to whatever means were at hand for working upon the superstitions of their public. In an age peculiarly prone to belief in witchcraft and devilry of all kinds, they established a pre-eminence as exorcists which assured to them a reputation even among Protestant populations. The organisation of the female

Capuchines, established at Naples in 1538 by a Catalan lady, appears to have been modelled upon the rigorous original rule of the Clares.

An even more striking contrast is that between the Capuchins and the Theatines, confirmed by Clement VII. *The Theatines.* in 1524, and soon settled on the Monte Pincio at Rome. Their founders were Gaetano of Thiene, a native of Vicenza, and Gian Pietro Caraffa. The former had quitted a lucrative post at the Roman court in order to transplant the ideas of the Oratory of the Divine Love to his native city, Venice and Verona, and had gradually come to concentrate his pious thoughts upon the reformation of the *secular* clergy of the Church. On his return to Rome, Bonifacio da Colle, a Lombard lawyer, became interested in his design, and then it was enthusiastically taken up by Caraffa, whose bishopric of Chieti, or, according to the older form, Theate, gave its name to the new Order of the *Theatines*.[1] The members of this order called themselves, not monks, but clerks-regular; their superior bore the title of provost; their costume was the ordinary clerical dress; their statutes explicitly declared it unfit that, either in the conduct of life or the services of religion, the conscience should be bound by mere usage. Clearly, the idea of their founders was the restoration of the clergy, by the example of these simple priests, to the primitive apostolic type. Indeed, the Theatines might remind us of the Low German Brotherhood of the Common Life, were it not for the select and aristocratic character impressed upon this

---

[1] Fra Paolo states that it was customary in his day at Venice to call 'votaresses of the Jesuits' *Chietines.*

'seminary of bishops' by Caraffa, who for a time gave himself up entirely to its cause. They showed great activity both in the care of the sick and as preachers, and their missions afterwards spread from Italy, where they were zealous in staying the growth of heresy, to the remote regions of Georgia, Circassia, and Tartary.

The example of the Theatines was imitated in several quarters. The clerks-regular of St. Paul (Paulines), <small>Other Orders in Italy.</small> whose congregation was founded by Antonio Maria Zacharia of Cremona and two Milanese associates in 1532, approved by Clement VII. in 1533, and confirmed as independent by Paul III. in 1534, in 1545 took the name of Barnabites, from the church of St Barnabas, which was given up to them at Milan. The Barnabites, who have been described as the democratic wing of the Theatines, actively engaged in the conversion of heretics both in Italy and in France and in that home of heresy, Bohemia. In 1540 Paul III. confirmed the order of the Somascines, so named from the town of Somasca. Their founder, a Venetian noble commonly called Girolamo Miani, appalled by the ravages of war in Lombardy, had consecrated his life and wealth to the service of the poor, and in particular of homeless children, and had founded several hospitals in this part of Italy. Both these traditions were carried on by his order, afterwards called the Order of St. Majolus, from a church made over to it at Padua; but it does not appear to have acquired a more than local importance. Almost equally modest in their beginnings were the labours of Philip of Neri, a young Florentine of good birth (1515–1595);

canonised 1622), who in 1548 instituted at Rome the Society of the Holy Trinity, to minister to the wants of the pilgrims at Rome. But the operations of his mission gradually extended till they embraced the spiritual welfare of the Roman population at large, and the reformation of the Roman clergy in particular. No figure is more serene and more sympathetic to us in the history of the Catholic reaction than that of this latter-day 'apostle of Rome.' From his association, which followed the rule of St. Augustine, sprang in 1575 the Congregation of the Oratory at Rome, famous as the seminary of much that is most admirable in the labours of the Catholic clergy.

This activity in the foundation and renovation of monastic orders continued throughout the reign of Paul III., whom in 1544 we find confirming the famous female order of the Ursulines, established by Angela of Brescia, with a view, not to isolation from the world, but to a living care of the unfortunate. There seems no reason for assuming any very close or direct connection to have existed in these years be-

*And Spain.*

tween the movement in Italy and the early efforts of Spanish mysticism. This altogether indigenous growth never exhibited the slightest tendency to estrange itself from the established Church, which, notwithstanding the fears of the Inquisition, was immeasurably strengthened by the encouragement communicated to pious minds from this new world of religious emotion. Peter of Alcantara (1499–1562) was one of the first to exhibit the combination of meditative religiosity with reforming enthusiasm characteristic of the Spanish mystics. Forced by John III.

of Portugal from the lovely conventual retreat in which he composed his *Golden Book* on mental prayer, he reformed the Franciscan order of which he was provincial in Estramadura, both in Spain and in Portugal, and in 1555 established the congregation of the Barefooted Friars, afterwards known as of the strictest observance of St. Peter of Alcantara. Alejo Venegas was likewise at the height of his activity in the period covered by the pontificate of Paul III., as were Juan d'Avilla (1500-69), the eloquent 'apostle of Andalusia,' and his Portuguese convert called Juan di Dio, who in 1540 founded the order of the Brethren of Charity, devoted more especially to the relief of the physical sufferings of the poor and unhappy. To the same period and group belongs the Franciscan Juan de los Angeles, the friend of St. Francis of Borgia; but it was not till the next generation that the fruits of their enthusiasm were to become most fully manifest.

In Spain, the assistance given to the progress of the Counter-Reformation by these new associations was, from the nature of the case, wholly indirect; but, even as to Italy, an estimate of the extent of that assistance is not in all cases possible. The great religious society of which it remains to speak may be said to have been expressly called into life in order to advance the movement, which acquired an entirely new impetus so soon as it was informed by the fiery spirit of Spanish religious enthusiasm. The story of Ignatius Loyola (1491-1556), the founder of the Jesuit order, who, after his beatification had been pronounced by Pope Paul V. (1607), was canonised as St. Ignatius by Gregory

*The Company of Jesus.*

XV. (1622), cannot be narrated here. As has frequently been pointed out, such a character as Loyola's, and such a life's work as his, could have taken their origin nowhere but in Spain, the land of ardent aspirations and of heroic endurance, and from of old a nursery of combatant Christian chivalry. Even scholastic philosophy was not cultivated with pre-eminent success in mediæval Spain, and the mysticism to which reference has been made was the product of sentiment rather than of speculation. The *alumbrados*, though decried as a sect by ignorance and prejudice, were guiltless either of heretical intentions or of doctrinal independence. Thus the great religious revival of Ferdinand and Isabella had been carried out on a well-prepared soil, and its effects were enhanced by the conquest of the New World for the Cross as well as for the Crown. Lastly, though neither Ferdinand nor his grandson Charles would ever have deigned to become the mere tools of the Papacy, the nation was fully aware of their design that the power of Spain should control the world over which the Pope claimed the spiritual supremacy. Loyola accordingly lived in an atmosphere of ideas which forbade his being content with one more attempt at puritanising the Franciscan or some other of the older orders, or even with ranging himself among the Theatines (who gave him shelter at Venice in 1537), as one of Caraffa's saints suited for bishoprics. To the Theatines he no doubt owed the suggestion of such a society as that which he was on the eve of founding, but the idea had its roots in his nation's historic past.

When, on his partial recovery from his wound and

his surgeons, Loyola resolved to serve God and His saints as a monk, he cannot have known much about the progress of the Protestant Reformation. Indeed, when, after his ascetic exercises and visions in the Dominican convent at Manrese, and his infructuous pilgrimage to Jerusalem, he sat with heroic doggedness among the philosophy and divinity students at Alcala and Salamanca, though already himself in some measure a popular teacher and a counsellor of beautiful souls, the Inquisition twice laid hands upon him. Of course he was suspected of being an *alumbrado*. When in 1528 he resumed his studies at Paris, he must have felt nearer to the purpose of his life, with which his journeys into Belgium and to London may have had some connexion. At all events, before, in 1535, he betook himself to Venice, the nucleus of his great institution was in existence. At first it consisted of two academical acquaintances of Loyola, the Savoyard Pierre Le Fèvre and the noble Navarrese Francis Xavier, who then occupied a chair in the College of Beauvais at Paris. The Spaniards Lainez, Salmeron, and Bobadilla, and the Portuguese Rodriguez, likewise took part in the famous meeting held in the Church of St. Mary on Montmartre (August 15, 1534). The list was completed by the Savoyard Le Jay and the Frenchmen Codure and Brousset, all of them Parisian students, who, in the same or the following year, joined Loyola's followers during his own absence from Paris. In 1537 all the associates met first at Venice, and, towards the end of the year, at Rome. Already before they reached the latter city, their leader seems to have bestowed on them the name of the Company of Jesus, very possibly

C. H.

a reminiscence of one of the abortive religious orders of knighthood founded by Pius II. (1459), and always preferred by Loyola, as significant of the military organisation of his institution.[1] When, after their arrival at Rome, they found that the Holy Land remained inaccessible to them, they lost no time in defining to themselves the objects of their common engagements. Mission-work, especially among heretics, and afterwards among heathen, and education, were their special tasks. Thus, even before the confirmation of the order, probably about the time when Loyola was himself involved in charges of heresy, which are rather obscurely mixed up with his reprobation of the crypto-Lutheranism of a certain Piemontese monk, his followers distinguished themselves as the assailants of heresy at Rome itself, and at Ferrara and some of the neighbouring cities. Two members of the band were appointed to chairs of divinity at the *Sapienza*, while others were soon placed in charge of some of the schools recently founded by the Pope. But though Paul III. personally favoured the plans of Loyola, a protracted struggle ensued, which must have been conducted by the latter with singular skill, before the desired confirmation was granted. As has been the case with other eminent fanatics, the astute element in him showed itself comparatively late; but of its strength, his dealings with

---

[1] It was not the custom during the sixteenth century for individual members of the Society to call themselves 'Jesuits;' indeed, the term seems to be used as a kind of nickname, and is so employed by Calvin in 1560. In Spain and Portugal the members of the Company were, in its early days, known as Theatines, Ignatians, or Apostles.

temporal governments and their interests, as well as his injunctions to his disciples, leave no doubt. In the days of expectancy, though for a time the new religious enterprise was chiefly popular with the lower orders, yet it had also secured powerful friends, such as Cardinals Contarini and De Carpi, and the Emperor's sister, Margaret of Parma. Thus the Pope, upon whom a personal interview with Loyola had made a deep impression, was encouraged to ignore an unfavourable report from a commission of three cardinals, and on September 27, 1540, he issued the bull *Regimini*, confirming the new order. The subsequent bull, *Injunctum nobis* (1543), abolished the restriction of the number of the members of the order to sixty, which Loyola had speedily discovered a way of evading. New privileges facilitating the ministrations of the Company in all parts of the world were conferred upon it by Paul III. (1545 and 1549), while the results of its labours were amply recognised in his bull *Pastoralis officii cura* (1548). The Jesuits obtained all the rights of the older orders, together with the privilege for their general of absolving his subordinates from all ecclesiastical penalties except in abnormal cases reserved for the decision of the Pope. Other favours were granted to the order by Paul's successor, Julius III., who proved its consistent friend (1550).

The bulls establishing the order and extending its privileges contained in themselves the substance of the *Constitutions*, which, though not published till after the death of Loyola, and then as revised by Lainez (1558), had for some years previously

Its system.

regulated the life and labours of the Jesuits. With these were published the *Declarations*, which already exemplify the well-known Jesuit tendency to exceptions mitigating, and often to all appearance materially modifying, a rule. This tendency is carried much further in the collection of so-called *Secret Institutions* (*Monita Secreta*), from successive generals to their subordinates (first published in 1612), of which, however, the Jesuits have always denied the genuineness, and which, at all events, possesses no official character. On the other hand, there has been no attempt to gainsay Loyola's authorship of the *Spiritual Exercises*, published in 1548 for the use of laymen and novices, and to some extent suggested by a mystical manual of devotion by Garcia de Cisneros, abbot of Manrese. (The *Directory* for the conduct of these exercises was not definitively adopted till 1593–94.) From these sources we derive our knowledge of the principles and methods which were characteristic of the order in its early days, and by adhering to which it accomplished a great part of its successes.

In the three vows taken by an ordinary member of the Company there was nothing unfamiliar to common monastic usage. The simple import of the vow of poverty was indeed materially modified in practice, the Constitutions as well as the Declarations making sufficient provision in this direction; but in substance such had also been the case with earlier orders. Even as to the vow of obedience, Loyola could not in the way of metaphor go beyond the famous *perinde ac cadaver*, borrowed by him from St. Francis of Assisi. To this principle, as determining the relations of the members of the Company to their superiors, and to the general above all, the founder is, however, never weary of returning, and he is always ready, both in theory and in practice, to push it to its utmost logical consequences. Hence sprang the rule that in Europe no member of the Company should accept high office in the Church as bishop, archbishop, or cardinal. This rule owed its origin to the offer of the see of Trieste to Le Jay, and was enforced by Loyola, though with characteristic modifications, when that of Vienna was pressed upon Canisius.[1] Nor was even a virtual independence conceded by the general to the leading members of the order; he broke the attempt at resistance of Rodriguez when provincial in Portugal (1552), and taught even Lainez, in whom he must have divined his successor, to know his place (1543). Great importance no doubt also attached to the additional vow of obedience to the Pope in missionary matters, taken by the so-called professed of the four vows. But the members of the order who rose to this rank were few in number, amounting, it is said, to not more than thirty-five at the time of Loyola's death, and on an average to not more than two in the hundred of the entire body. In truth the success of the Company was much more largely than that of most other orders due to its chiefs or aristocracy. For though at first sight the enormous authority of the general might seem to give a monarchical character to the whole system, this authority was, in fact, the reverse of limited. The assistants, representing the chief provinces, and forming a kind of cabinet under the

[1] The first Jesuit who accepted the purple was Toletus (Francisco de Toledo), s.a. 1593.

general, had not only the right of assembling a general congregation of the order in his despite, but in a case of urgency might proceed to his deposition by a still more summary method. Loyola himself was about two years before his death (30th July 1556) obliged to accept a vicar imposed upon him by his assistants. A constitution of this kind leaves room for much suspicion and intrigue, but in the vigilance thus engendered lay another of the vital principles of the Jesuit system of administration and life. In many of its members the system, hinging on obedience and guarded at every point by *surveillance*, may have crushed some of the most powerful as well as most generous motives of human action, but it would be an error to regard the whole institution as a machine worked by a single will. The early activity of the Jesuits, though intense, was hardly so multiplicitous as that of some other orders. It was, as observed, chiefly directed to missionary and propagandistic labours, including the diplomacy of the Company, largely worked through the confessors of royal and princely personages, and to education,—soon in the main to its higher branches only. But all its seeds were sown and watered and all its fruits gathered *ad majorem Dei gloriam,* that is to say, for the ulterior purposes which the Society covered by this phrase, viz., the benefit of the Church as represented by the Papacy. What in Protestant eyes gives so indescribable a hollowness to Jesuit theology and Jesuit education, even to Jesuit oratory and literature and art, is precisely what attests the subordination in this system of everything to the purpose for which it was called into life. It is not wonderful that no other religious society should have been trusted so much and hated so bitterly. That the Company of Jesus has in general remained free from outward extravagances of zeal such as have often given offence in other religious associations, is largely due to the cosmopolitan character impressed on it by its founder. Already his early followers were by him as much as possible employed on missions to countries other than their own, while his plan of frequently changing the place of sojourn of the members of his company emancipated them from the routine which impairs activity.[1]

Nothing, accordingly, is more striking in the early history of the Jesuits than the zeal and promptitude with which from the very beginning of their formal existence as a community each of them addressed himself to his specific share of their work. At Easter 1541, Ignatius Loyola, with some little coyness, accepted the generalship, to which he had been elected by six professed members of the order, and proceeded to the formal distribution of its labours. Almost the first mission intrusted to members of the order was that on which, in the same year, 1541, Pasquier-Brouet and Salmeron, accompanied by the apostolic notary Zapata as a novice, set out by way of Scotland to Ireland, where, in 1542, they spent a month of extreme and apparently futile hazards. Yet these same men had a large share in the campaign against heresy which was waged

*Its early progress.*

*In Italy.*

[1] The order was as early as 1547 relieved by Papal ordinance from the control of female conventuals. In 1545 Loyola had sanctioned an association of Jesuitesses, but he soon found reason to change his mind. The experiment was renewed and again suppressed under Urban VIII. (1631).

in Northern and Central Italy in the period immediately ensuing (1542–43). We are informed by Jesuit historiographers that Pasquier-Brouet recovered Foligno for the Church (1542–43); that Salmeron was victorious at Modena and Montepulciano (1543); while Lainez, after working with Le Fèvre at Parma and Piacenza, stemmed the tide of error at Venice, where, as elsewhere, it was among the upper classes that the teaching of the Jesuits proved most immediately effective, and where they founded a college (1542). But above all, our attention is directed to the success of their efforts in these years at Faenza, whence, in the course of a prolonged campaign, which established them in a kind of acknowledged control over the inhabitants, they caused the arch-heretic Ochino himself to withdraw (1543–45). Shortly afterwards (1546), they established a college at Bologna. There is no reason to contest either the zeal or the success of this home mission of the Jesuits, whose labours, however, coincided with the reorganisation of the Inquisition at Rome (1542). Even at Naples they established a footing through Salmeron. At Rome itself, which, in accordance with the design of the order, was its permanent centre, Loyola in 1550 established the *Collegium Romanum*, soon afterwards removed to the site of the well-known *Gesù*; and two years later the foundation of the *Collegium Germanicum*, approved by a bull of Pope Julius III., offered visible testimony to the missionary aspirations of the Society in reference to what might be called the least secure part of Europe.

Spain.  In Spain the progress of the Company seemed at first less assured, though during the first decade of its existence it was mainly composed of Spaniards, who furnished nearly three-quarters of the first general congregation of the order. But, apart from the manifest unwillingness of Loyola to give a national colour to his institution, the Jesuit revival might well at first seem to the people, and more especially to the clergy of Spain, the mere surplusage of an accepted religious movement. The episcopate and the universities were alike under the influence of the Dominicans, the chief agents of the Inquisition. Finally, the sovereign of Spain, who was also, in point of fact, the supreme governor of the Church in his dominions, had no love to spare for the protegees of the Pope. Thus it came to pass that in Spain the Jesuits were for a time thought neither very interesting nor at all respectable. But before very long, the inner affinity between the order and the nation from which it had sprung prevailed, and the efforts of Araoz provoked great enthusiasm in Castile, Catalonia, and the Basque provinces. It was through his agency that Francis Borgia, Duke of Gandia, the viceroy of Catalonia, was induced to accord his powerful support to the order, whose permanent establishment in Spain was virtually due to him. In 1548 he became himself a member of the Company, of which he afterwards rose to be general (1565-72); and in the same year, Alcala having been already deeply impressed by the preaching of Villanueva, Salamanca became the seat of a Jesuit college. More rapid was the early progress of the Jesuits in Portugal, where, under John III., they attained to the highest influence, and whence Xavier early (1541) set forth

*Portugal.*

for India, to earn for himself the sacred title of its apostle. Rodriguez, who remained behind, superintended the foundation (1542) of the famous college of the order at Coimbra; and being himself member of a noble Portuguese family, was intrusted with the education of John's successor, Sebastian, whose mind he helped to imbue with a deep, and, as it proved, fatal religious enthusiasm. The example thus given of the influence obtainable by the education of a prince was not lost upon the Company; though Philip II., who, after Sebastian's death (1578), had made himself master of unwilling Portugal (1580), never forgave the Jesuits the influence which they had exerted there under the last two national sovereigns, and which they continued to exert under his own rule.

In France, on the other hand, notwithstanding its early association with Paris, the Company had to contend with many difficulties. It was here regarded as an essentially Spanish growth; moreover, during some of these years (1542-44) France was again at war with Spain. Under Henry II. the order enjoyed the goodwill of the crown and of the Cardinal of Lorraine; but both the Parliament of Paris and the University strongly resisted a royal ordinance sanctioning the establishment of a Jesuit college in the capital (1550), and an agitation was provoked which, after a formal condemnation had been pronounced by the Sorbonne (1554), spread throughout the country, and for a time almost entirely stopped the labours of the order there. According to Jesuit historians, the dismissal from the Company of Postel, whom Margaret of Valois called the Wonder of the World, contributed to this result (1551); but of its general nature there can be no doubt. The jealous pride of the university, the national instincts of the bishops and other clergy, and the mocking spirit abroad among the people, were the real obstacles in the way of the Society, whose members were only here and there tolerated in the realm until the beginning of the great religious wars warned the friends of the Papacy to conciliate its most consistent champions (1561). After this the fortunes of the order in France varied, but the national antipathy against it never came to an end. Of all the generals who have ruled over it, not one has been a Frenchman.

In the neighbouring Low Countries the progress of the Jesuits was likewise slow, though at first Le Fèvre gained a following in the University of Louvain. Even after the resignation of Charles V., it was only by slow degrees that Philip II. was prevailed upon to admit them into the country (1556). They were, however, greatly favoured by the regent, Margaret of Parma, upon whom they exercised a direct influence through her confessor; and thus their colleges at Louvain and Antwerp were opened, and the former place in particular became a centre of their operations.

<small>The Netherlands.</small>

In Germany their success was continuous in the Catholic parts of the Empire. As early as 1540 Le Fèvre arrived in the capacity of theologian to the imperial ambassador at Worms, whence he proceeded to Ratisbon. His reports made a great impression upon the Pope, and probably did more to stimulate propagandist efforts than was effected

<small>Germany.</small>

by the religious conferences in the direction of re-union.
On Le Fèvre's removal to Spain, he was succeeded in
Germany by Le Jay and Bobadilla, of whom the latter
had in Italy laboured in common with Cardinal Pole
at Viterbo. The political difficulties of their task began when, after the Smalcaldic war, Charles V. sought
to impose the Augsburg *Interim* (1548) upon the
Empire. Bobadilla had to be recalled as a sacrifice
to the displeasure excited in Charles by his successful
exertions in urging the Catholic princes to refuse
acceptance for themselves of the compromise, onesided and temporary as it was. On the other hand,
greater confidence than ever was felt in the Jesuits by
the orthodox Duke William IV. of Bavaria (1508-50),
whose example was, after some hesitation, followed
by his successor, Albert V. (1550-79.) Under
him, as will be seen, Ingolstadt, though it never became a purely Jesuit university like Innsbruck and
Dillingen, was to a great extent given up to the order.
Into the hereditary dominions of the house of Austria
the Jesuits effected an entry in 1552, when King
Ferdinand invited to Vienna two Jesuits from Ingolstadt, Peter Canisius (Kanes), rector of the university, and his companion Nicholas Gandamus. Canisius
had already done good service at Cologne during the
struggle against the Archbishop Hermann of Wied,
in which the Church ultimately proved victorious
(1547), and soon obtained considerable influence over
King Ferdinand. From Vienna, where he held an
important position both in the university and in the
community at large, he undertook a series of special
missions in Upper and Lower Austria, and supplied

the *Collegium Germanicum* at Rome with promising novices. In Bohemia, where their influence was to be so momentous at a later stage of the country's history, the Jesuits first arrived in 1556, and, in defiance of public opinion, maintained their hold upon the *Clementinum*, their college at Prague, and upon the churches which gradually fell into their hands. In Hungary the settlement which they effected in 1561 was merely transitory.

Such had been the progress of his Company in this part of Europe, that, not long before his death, Loyola resolved upon the foundation of an Upper German province, at the head of which Canisius was placed (1556). It was he who, at the religious conference held at Worms in 1557, destroyed such illusions as still remained concerning a possible reconciliation between Roman and Protestant doctrine, and who pursued the same line of argument at Trent. When he resigned his provincialate in 1569, he had contributed more than any other man to transform the spirit of German Catholicism into one of unyielding intolerance. The text-book of the preachers and teachers whom his energy had planted through Upper Germany was his *Summa Doctrinæ Christianæ* (1554), which is said, in the first hundred and thirty years after its publication, to have run through four hundred editions.

Canisius' visit to Poland in 1558, when he reported the country deeply infected with heresy, led to no
<small>Poland, &c.</small> positive result, nor was it till after the close of the Council of Trent that the order was established in this kingdom (1564). Its entry into Sweden belongs to a still later phase of the religious reaction. At the time of the death of Loyol,

(1556), the order numbered something like one thousand members, who were distributed through thirteen provinces. Of these provinces, the majority were Spanish or Portuguese, or formed out of the colonial possessions of these kingdoms; three Italian, one French, two German. The formation of one of the last named, however, which was to have its nucleus in the Low Countries, still awaited the approval of Philip II., while the objects as well as the methods of the founder of the order were clearly marked out for his successors. They well knew that, apart from the distant missions to which Xavier had, up to his death (1552), devoted himself in India, Japan, and China, their work must be carried on in even wider orbits than it had been under their founder, and that, above all, they must never cease to act on the offensive. Lainez, the second general of the order, was fully adequate to the task; with Loyola's boldness, energy, and astuteness he combined the subtlety of mind which enabled him to give to Jesuit theology an elasticity of its own, while holding it fast to its cardinal principles, including the infallibility and the universal episcopacy of the Pope. The subsequent history of the Church of Rome by no means uniformly shows the Papacy in harmony with the Jesuits, but it very rarely shows the latter inconsistent with themselves, or with their task of compelling Christendom to turn back with them.

*The order at the time of Loyola's death.*

In the contest now waged by Rome she had resort to the old as well as to the new engines in her arsenal. Like the Jesuit order, towards which it long continued unfriendly, the Inquisition in its modern form was

Spanish in origin. From Aragon, where the institution had, with an eye to the wealth of Judaising Christians, been revived on the basis of a union of authority between the Dominicans and laymen in the confidence of the crown, it had reached Castile, and under Ferdinand and Isabella it had flourished throughout Spain, and had extended to Majorca and Sardinia. Early in the sixteenth century it had been forced upon the Sicilians; but at Naples a successful resistance had been offered to its introduction. During the whole of this period the attitude of the Papacy towards the Inquisition had been neither sympathetic nor the reverse. The spirit of the Renascence age, and the absence of any current of religious feeling strong enough to overwhelm political considerations, produced in the Papal governments of this period an unmistakable spirit of tolerance; but the financial advantages to be gained from the renewed organism sanctioned by Sixtus IV. could not escape his successors. Hence the frequent conflict between Papal engagements towards the most Catholic sovereigns and Papal exemptions granted to those upon whom the judgment of the Inquisition was, with the eager concurrence of these sovereigns, about to descend; hence reclamations, reservations, and disappointments hardly less cruel than the tender mercies of Torquemada. After some early struggles, Spain pressed the instrument of her sufferings closer and closer into her flesh, resenting repeated Papal attempts to mitigate its severity; nor were the efforts of its agents or the sufferings of its victims diminished under the sway of Ximenez (1507–18), although this great man was not blind to the Chris-

*The Inquisition in Spain:*

tian principle underlying the common saw as to prevention and cure. Under Adrian, who succeeded Ximenez as Inquisitor-General, the combined jealousy of King, Cortes, and Pope threatened the Inquisition with the loss of a great part of its powers; but the temper of Charles was changed by the revolt of the Castilian cities, and the Inquisition came forth from this season of trial with its strength unimpaired. During his five years of office the hand of the good Adrian was as heavy upon the culprits as that of any of his predecessors had been; and it is probably an estimate below the fact according to which, during the forty-three years of the first four Inquisitors-General, the Spanish Inquisition burnt more than 18,000 persons, besides putting over 9000 to death in *effigie*, and sentencing over 206,000 to divers non-capital penalties. To Adrian was also due the establishment of the tribunal of the Inquisition in the East Indies and in the New World.

On the appointment (1523) of Adrian's successor, Manrique, archbishop of Seville and afterwards cardinal, hopes were entertained of a more lenient conduct of the Inquisition. Towards the Morescoes there was indeed an occasional show of politic moderation, though in the main the Inquisition worked steadily towards the expulsion of the entire Moorish population from Spanish soil, which, when accomplished (1609), permanently impoverished the country. But there was no general relaxation of activity or rigour, and at the time of Manrique's death (1538), although Charles V. had temporarily deprived its jurisdiction of certain privileges, the Inquisition had spread a network of not less than nineteen provincial tribunals over Spain and her colonies, and had established itself (1536) across the frontier in Portugal. This was the period in which Lutheran books first found their way across the Pyrenees; but it is as yet only outside their own country that Spaniards such as Juan Valdez and his brother Alfonso, or again such as Alfonso Ligurio and Michael Servetus, are found in sympathy with, or even in advance of, the ideas of the Reformation. Under the generalate next but one to Manrique's, that of Fernando Valdez, archbishop of Seville (1547–66), the Spanish Inquisition assumed the stereotyped form belonging to it as an agency of the Counter-Reformation. From the time when Philip II. solemnly undertook the protection of the Inquisition at the famous *auto da fé* of Valladolid (October 8, 1559), he completely identified himself with the institution; but already Charles V. had in his last years become a convert to the methods as well as to the principles of the inquisitors, although he wished their name to be eschewed in Flanders, and although he had formerly for a time curtailed their jurisdiction in Spain. Both sovereigns contrived to put the Inquisition to very useful governmental purposes; but above all, the religious uniformity at which it aimed seemed to them the surest guarantee of political as well as of religious unity. Thus protected and fostered by the temporal power, and furnished with new powers and privileges by Pope Paul IV. (1555–59), the Inquisition crushed Protestantism out of Spain, where about the middle of the century its roots were probably more widely spread than has been sometimes supposed. Its chief centres seem to have been Seville and Valladolid. In the former, Rodrigo de Valer, a young nobleman impassioned by the enthusiasm of moral conversion, was confined in a convent, where he died. Among men of learning charged with heretical tendencies, Ægidius (J. Gil) recanted; Ponce de la Fuente died in prison. At Valladolid the establishment of a Protestant community is ascribed to Carlos de Seso, and thence these opinions spread to the neighbouring parts of Castile and Leon. Those who undertake the laborious task of accurately following the merciless winnowing-machine in its operations may perhaps succeed in distinguishing between the prosecutions of Lutherans, Calvinists, *alumbrados*, and *dejados* (Quietists), which filled the archives of the Spanish Inquisition. On the one hand, it flattered the national pride by scorning all consideration for the foreigner, who, whether ambassador, or merchant, or common mariner, found himself subjected to its control, and often exposed to its penalties. On the other, it excited that official self-consciousness which made a Lope de Vega take pride in placing his style of 'Familiar of the Office' upon the title-pages of his books, by showing perfect fearlessness of either temporal greatness or spiritual dignity, and by subjecting to the processes of its examiners princes, prelates, ministers of state, and members of religious orders. Indeed, the chief concern of its operations was with the clerical world; from archbishops and bishops, such as, above all, Carranza, archbishop of Toledo, who, on account of his 'Commentaries on the Christian Catechism' (1558), was subjected to an arrest of seventeen years' duration, not interrupted even by the declaration in his favour of the Council of Trent, to supposed irregulars such as Ignatius Loyola and Teresa de Jesus. These examples sufficiently show how imperfect was the harmony between the movement of the Counter-Reformation as a whole and the Spanish Inquisition, albeit they so largely made war on common adversaries.

Reference will be made below to the attempt of Philip II. (1559) to introduce into the Netherlands a *The Netherlands.* system by which, in enquiries into matters of faith, the bishop of each diocese was to be assisted by two *inquisitors*, in addition to seven canons—an attempt so well remembered even in the Catholic provinces that they had no scruple in recording their renunciation of it in the Pacification of Ghent (1576), which secured to the Church her exclusive privileges in the south. In the neighbouring *France.* kingdom of France the zealous party were, in the reign of Henry II., anxious to introduce the Inquisition when they found the ordinary tribunals unwilling to apply the powers conferred upon them for the suppression of heresy; but the Parliament of Paris defeated both their first attempt (1555) and another which was supported by a Papal bull approved by a royal declaration (1557). The Cardinal of Lorraine indeed prevailed upon Henry II. to force the Parliament to register the edict establishing the Inquisition (1558), but it remained ineffective, largely by reason of the king's political relations with the German Protestant princes. In the brief reign of Francis II., during which the Guise family controlled the government, the edict of Romorantin (May 1559) went far towards establishing a system like that of the Spanish Inquisition in France, and a board of four cardinals was appointed; but the death of the young king (December) cut short their operations.

In Naples the viceroy of Charles VI., the unyielding Pedro de Toledo, was, at the suggestion of Caraffa, now archbishop of the province, instructed to renew the attempt to introduce the Inquisition (1546). It failed again; but when once more, and more effectually, repeated eighteen years later, the institution had already become a national one, and could about the same time (1563-64) be imposed upon the Milanese with the direct co-operation of Rome. When the Papacy had at last adopted the revived Inquisition as part of its regular machinery of government, the headquarters of the institution were logically transferred to Rome itself. In the opinion of Caraffa, and those who like him regarded the extirpation of heresy as the primary task of the Church, the counsels of the reforming cardinals needed supplementing by measures which directly addressed themselves to this end; and thus, in July 1542, Paul III. issued the bull *Licet ab initio*, constituting the Congregation of the Holy Office at Rome. It consisted of six cardinals, and received unrestricted powers of enquiry and punishment, with a sphere of jurisdiction in theory equally unlimited. Care was, however, taken to assure the chiefs of the Spanish Inquisition that no prejudice was intended to their authority. Caraffa was, in the first instance, placed at the head of the Congregation, with other Dominicans by his side; but the institution is said to have had the approval of Loyola. Its effect on the religious life of Italy was great, especially after the stringency of its proceedings had been increased by Caraffa on his elevation to the Papacy as Paul IV., and again by Pius V., after an interval of comparative moderation. The statement that, after the death of the last-named Pope (1572), no capital punishment was inflicted in the states of the Church on account of religious charges, is incorrect; but the instances in which the penalty of death was inflicted by the Roman Inquisition were beyond dispute comparatively few. The numbers of its victims were not here, as in Spain, swelled by two ill-fated large alien nationalities, but were made up entirely of those suspected of Protestant views, or of the various shades of skepsis, classed together under the convenient name of atheism. Both Lutheranism and Calvinism incontestably counted numerous adherents in the towns of almost every part of Italy; moreover, the tendency to independence of religious thought must have received some encouragement from the infusion of a strong element of liberalism into the composition of the Sacred College. The men in whom a popular Italian reformation movement, had such a thing been possible, might have found its natural leaders, fled for their lives from the Inquisition, taking refuge at the very hearths of the heresies which it denounced. Bernardino Ochino, after many adventures, reached Switzerland, which, with other Protestant countries, sheltered him for the long remainder of his life (to 1568). Peter-Martyr (Vermigli), summoned like him to Rome, likewise found a refuge at Geneva, whence he afterwards passed for a time to England. Many other suspects of less note hastened across the Alps, and behind them the storm broke over the communities to which they had belonged. At Lucca it proved possible to resist the efforts of the Inquisition to establish a permanent tribunal there. The surrender of Burlamacchi to the Emperor, who put him to death (1548), was primarily the consequence of his revolutionary political designs; but such was not the case with the victims found at Ferrara (from 1551) and Bologna (1553). These proceedings belong to the pontificate of Julius III., but already under Paul III. the Seignory of Venice had consented to establish an inquisitorial tribunal, into which care was taken to introduce lay representatives of the government, but which resorted to measures of considerable severity, including, as is stated, the execution of nineteen sentences of death at Vicenza, Treviso, and Bergamo (from 1548). But neither at Venice herself, and at the University of Padua, nor in the other subject towns, were Protestant sympathies extinguished, so that after the accession of Paul IV. the rigour of the tribunal was revived, and several Venetians charged with heresy were delivered up to the Pope and burnt at Rome. Elsewhere in Italy, as already observed, the activity of the Inquisition increased under Paul IV. and Pius V. But in truth it was now a self-working organism, and its pressure was often surest where it was slowest, as in the melancholy case of the Duchess Renée of Ferrara (1584).

The Spanish Inquisition, of which the Roman may be regarded as a branch, could not have prevailed in Italy without the political ascendancy of Spain, which neither temporal nor spiritual authorities, including that of the Popes themselves, could refuse to acknowledge. Such brutalities as the massacre of the Waldenses at Guardia in Calabria (1562), which Philibert Emmanuel of Savoy would, if he could, have emulated in his raid upon the Waldenses of the Alps, were the excesses of this foreign despotism; but its iron entered into the heart of the Italian people at large, even outside the parts of the country directly under Spanish sway. The selfish greed of foreign nations had delivered over Italy to the doom of political dependence; now the Spanish rule and ascendancy likewise took away from her sons and daughters what remained to them of the spirit of moral and intellectual freedom, which, under other circumstances, might have survived the Renascence, or have added to it an ennobling phase.

In asserting, mainly through the medium of the Inquisition, her claim to a censorship over the literature and art of the Christian world, the Church of Rome stood on a well-trodden path. The system which, with the co-operation of the crown, Torquemada had practised with relentless zeal in Spain, and which in Germany, though set in motion after a much milder fashion, had covered the Dominicans of Cologne with undying ridicule, was developed in Spain under the inquisitorial administrations of Adrian and of Manrique, the latter of whom empowered his officers to excommunicate possessors or readers of heretical books, as well as those who had failed to denounce them. In this way it was hoped to extinguish many pernicious reputations, including the fame of Erasmus. No sooner had the revived Inquisition been formally

*The Index.*

established at Rome than Caraffa, as its official head, published an edict prohibiting, under the severest penalties short of death, the reading, purchase, or possession, as well as the printing or sale, of any heretical book, or of any anonymous work not expressly approved by the Sacred Office (1543). Not long before this (1539), Charles V., resolved, like Ferdinand and Isabella before him, to assert the secular authority in these matters, had prohibited on pain of death the circulation in Flanders of any of Luther's writings (1540), with the Papal approval charged the University of Louvain with the task of drawing up a list of books prohibited in Flanders; and after it had made its appearance (1546), the example was followed, and the list enlarged, by the Inquisition in Spain (1556). Both here and elsewhere decrees abounded establishing rigorous rules of censorship. The culminating ordinance was that of Philip II. (1558), attaching the penalties of death and confiscation of property to the reading, purchase, or possession of books prohibited by the Sacred Office. But the first *Index* of prohibited books published by Papal authority, and therefore, unlike the *catalogi* previously issued by royal, princely, or ecclesiastical authorities, valid for the whole Church, was that authorised by a bull of Paul IV. in 1559. In 1564 followed the *Index* published by Pius IV., as drawn up in harmony with the decrees of the Council of Trent, which, after all, appears to be a merely superficial revision of its predecessor. Other *Indices* followed, for which various authorities were responsible, the most important among them being the *Index Expurgatorius*, sanctioned by a bull of

Clement VIII. in 1595, which proved so disastrous to the great printing trade of Venice. After a time the prohibitions contained in these lists came to extend not only to particular books, but to particular passages in books. Thus one of the scholars employed on the so-called *Index Expurgatorius* of the Duke of Alva (1571) is said to have boasted that he had struck out 600 passages in ancient writers, all of which appeared to contradict the claims or doctrines of the Church of Rome. While the censors who conducted the execution of these ordinances in the several dioceses were jointly appointed by bishops and inquisitors, the final decision on all these matters was intrusted to the *Congregation of the Index* at Rome, which was technically independent of the Holy Office. But the spirit of the Inquisition pervaded an institution which, apart from the awkward perversity of its operations (illustrated by the history of the Jesuits from St. Francis Borgia to Bellarmine), ultimately tended not only to weaken the defensive powers of the Church of Rome, but to throw contempt upon them. Most lamentable of all was its effect upon that branch of the Church to which the spiritual element in the Counter-Reformation was so pre-eminently indebted. The fear which paralyses the tongue of the teacher and makes the pen drop from the scholar's hand narrowed and unmanned that Spanish Church whose representatives proved themselves in so many respects worthy of her past at the Council of Trent.

## CHAPTER III.

### *THE COUNCIL OF TRENT.*

THE conciliar idea, though discredited by the experience of the previous two pontificates, had by no means slumbered under either Adrian VI. or Clement VII. The former had not altogether rejected the German demand for a General Council, with which his imperial pupil from the first strenuously identified himself; on the other hand, Clement VII. had been driven to a variety of subterfuges in order to escape the necessity of convoking one himself. There is no reason to suppose that the promise of summoning a General Council made by Paul III. in his conclave was intended to deceive. His insight into the actual state of the Church must have made it clear to him that no means of bringing about systematic reforms in it could be so effective as a genuine representative assembly of the Church at large; and arguments to this end were eagerly addressed to him by Sadolet and other members of the party in the Sacred College, which for the time had his ear. Yet he, like his predecessor, feared to bring together an assembly whose decrees might be moulded by the imperial will, and was still more apprehensive of the attitude which

<small>Paul III., Charles V., and the Council.</small>

the council, if meeting under the conditions of freedom desired by the Germans, might assume towards the Protestant reformation. Charles V., however, continued urgent, more especially after he had abandoned the hope of restoring the religious unity of the Empire by force. Thus, with the view of meeting the Emperor's wish without putting the council and himself entirely into his hands, Paul III., in June 1536, actually published a bull summoning a council to Mantua for the coming year. But the Third War between Charles V. and Francis I. intervened (1536-38); and when, after its close, under further pressure and some measure of menace from the Emperor, the Pope ordered the council to assemble at Vicenza (May 1538), the meeting was again postponed. When the project was resumed in 1541, the progress made during the interval by Protestantism in Northern and Central Europe, and the hollowness of the religious truce patched up at Ratisbon, combined to impress the necessity of definitive action upon both Pope and Emperor. At their meeting at Lucca, the Pope agreed to summon a council for the close of the following year (November 1542) to Trent, a town situate within the Empire and in the Austrian dominions. Here Cardinals Morone and Pole actually made their appearance as Papal legates. But though the Emperor had likewise sent his ambassadors, Mendoza and Granvelle, events once more proved too strong for him: before the date fixed was reached he was involved in another war with France and her ally the Turk (1542-44), and in July 1543 the small assembly of prelates at Trent was dispersed by a bull of suspension.

The Peace of Crespy (September 1544), ominous of evil for the prospects of Protestantism, was immediately followed by a Papal bull summoning all the bishops of Christendom to Trent for March 15, 1545. At Rome the council was now known to be inevitable; but by whom would it be controlled, and what scope should be given to its deliberations? The Pope's eyes had been opened to the whole extent of the possibilities confronting the Church when at Speier in 1544 the Emperor had promised the Protestants to secure them a free council, or settle the religious question without further ado at a diet of the Empire. As to the French Church, notwithstanding the sound articles of faith recently enunciated by the Sorbonne (March 1543), there was little hope of overawing it except by a very decided attitude. This, again, was out of the question if, in accordance with the views of Cardinal Pole, the chief functions of the assembly over which he was once more called to preside, were to be the bringing back of the German Protestants into the fold, and the restoration of discipline in the Church at large. Paul III. was accordingly both well advised in summoning the council in earnest, and sagacious in choosing for the purpose the moment when Charles was concerting with Francis the suppression of the Protestants. The beginnings of the reorganisation of the Church had already proved the work of internal reform to be something more than the dream of a few enthusiasts; now if ever was the time for the Papacy to use a General Council for the advantage of the Church and of her directing power. Of Protestant importunity there need be no real fear. Luther had declared himself hopeless (1539) as to any real reformation of the Church through a council convened by the Pope. Henry VIII., whose alliance the German princes were wooing, had protested against the authority claimed for the Mantuan assembly (1536). Thus there is no reason for supposing Paul III. to have summoned the council on this occasion as a mere makeshift. Though the actions of this Pope were not as a rule dictated by pure religious enthusiasm, yet he had every reason for desiring a more distinct enunciation of those doctrines of the Church which she was now with renewed energy propagating among heathens and heretics, while at the same time using the occasion for a serious reformation of her discipline. So much, without prejudicing the Papal control over the Church, Paul III. may be credited with having wished to secure; nor was the result out of conformity with his wishes.

On December 13, 1545, the three legates appointed by the Pope held their public entry into Trent, and the council was formally opened. Paul III.'s continued desire to conciliate the Emperor was shown by his adherence to Trent as the locality of the council, when the legates again urged the choice of a town on Italian soil. Yet the very bishop of Trent, Cardinal Madruccio, was a prince of the Empire, and by descent attached to the house of Austria, whose interests he consistently erpresented during the first series of sessions. The Papal legates, with whose control over the council the Emperor at the outset showed no intention of interfering, typified the different elements in the ecclesiastical policy of Paul III. The presiding legate,

Cardinal del Monte (afterwards Pope Julius III.), while notable neither for religious zeal nor for wise self-control, was a thorough-going supporter of the interests of the Curia. Cardinal Cervino, afterwards Pope Marcellus II., a prelate of blameless life, was animated by those ideas of ecclesiastical reform of which Pope Paul had encouraged the open expression; but he was more especially eager for the extirpation of heresy, and not over-scrupulous in the choice of means for reaching his ends. Lastly, Cardinal Pole's presence at Trent, in which some have seen a mere Papal ruse, must have surrounded the early proceedings of the council with a hopeful glamour in the eyes of those who, like himself, expected from it the reunion as well as the reinvigoration of Western Christendom. Nothing, as had probably been foreseen at Rome, could have better facilitated the immediate establishment of the ascendancy in the council of the Papal policy than the composition of its opening meeting. Of the thirty-four ecclesiastics present, only five were Spanish and two French bishops, and no German bishop had crossed the Alps. Nor had any secular power except the Emperor and King Ferdinand sent their ambassadors. The business machinery of the council, which the legates lost no time in getting into order, was altogether in favour of their influence as managers. Learned doctors, without being, as in former councils, allowed to take part in the debates, prepared the work of the three committees or congregations, who in their turn brought it up for discussion to the general congregations. The sessions in which the decrees thus prepared were actually passed had a purely formal character, but before they were successively held opportunity enough was given for manipulation and delay. The voting in the council was by heads, instead of by nations, as at Constance and Basel; and care was taken to refresh by occasional additions the working majority of Italian bishops, mostly, in comparison with the 'ultramontane' prelates, holders of petty sees. Some of these are even stated to have bound themselves by a sworn engagement to uphold the interests of the Holy See, though by no means all of the Italian bishops were servile Curialists; witness those of Chioggia and of Fiesole. The council in its second session (January 7, 1546) waived the form of title by which previous councils had implicitly declared their representative authority paramount. On the other hand, it boded well for the cause of reform that, by an early resolution, virtually all abbots and members of the monastic orders except five generals were excluded. Clearly, episcopal interest was resolved upon asserting itself. So long, however, as the German bishops were detained in their dioceses by the duty of repressing heresy there, while the great body of the French were kept away by the vigilant jealousy of their government, the episcopal interest and the episcopal principle were mainly represented in the council by the Spanish prelates, the loyal subjects of Charles, and the convinced inheritors of the traditions of Ximenez. Their leader was Pacheco, cardinal of Jaën. With him came eminent theological professors, who in the early period of the council at least were without rivals—Dominico de Soto, whom Queen Mary afterwards placed in Peter Martyr's chair at Oxford, and Bartolomeo Carranza, afterwards primate of all Spain, and for many years a prisoner of the Inquisition. Through the Emperor's ambassador, the accomplished and indefatigable, but not invariably discreet, Mendoza, the Spanish bishops were carefully apprised of the wishes of their sovereign.

The crucial question as to the order in which the council should debate the two divisions of subjects which it had met to settle had to be decided at once; and the compromise arrived at showed both the strength of the minority and the unwillingness of the leaders of the majority, the presiding legates, to push matters to an extreme. Their instructions from the Pope were to give the declaration of dogma the preference over the announcement of disciplinary reforms; for it seemed to him of primary necessity to draw, while there was time, a clear line of demarcation between the Church and heresy; and for this, as he correctly judged, the assistance of the council was absolutely indispensable. The Emperor, on the other hand, was still unwilling to shut the door completely against the Protestants, while both he and the Episcopal party at the council were eager for that reformation of the life and government of the Church which seemed to them her most crying need. Ultimately it was agreed that the declaration of dogma and the reformation of abuses should be treated *pari passu*, the decrees formulated in each case being from time to time announced simultaneously. Taking into account the subsequent history of the council, one can hardly deny that this arrangement saved the work of the assembly from being left half done. Nor was the progress made in the period ending with the eighth session of the Council (11th March 1547), intrigues

*Order of business.*

and quarrels notwithstanding, by any means trifling. On the doctrinal side, the foundations of the faith were in the first instance examined, and the whole character of the doctrinal decrees of the council was in point of fact determined, when the authority of the tradition of the Church, including of course the decrees of her œcumenical councils, was acknowledged by the side of that of Scripture. Little to the credit of the council's capacity for taking pains, the authenticity of the Vulgate was proclaimed, a pious wish being added that it should be henceforth printed as correctly as possible.[1] At first, Pope Paul III. hesitated about giving his assent to these decrees, which had been passed before receiving his approval, and showed some anxiety to prevent a similar course being taken in the matter of discipline by publishing a regulatory bull on his own authority. But on being more fully advised by the legates of the nature of the situation, he consented to allow the debates to proceed, provided always that the decrees should be submitted to him before publication. During the next months (April–June 1546) the work of the council was accordingly vigorously continued in both its branches. In that of discipline, the episcopal and the monastic interests at once came into conflict on the subject of the license for preaching; and still more excitement was aroused by the question of episcopal residence, which brought into conflict the

<sub>Dogma.</sub>

<sub>Discipline.</sub>

---

[1] When, about forty years later (1590), this wish had been, after a fashion, carried into effect by Sixtus V., this authentic Latin Bible had, after all, to be promptly withdrawn, and a corrected but still not very correct edition substituted (1592).

highest purposes of the episcopal office and the selfish profits of the Roman Curia. The discussions on preaching ended with a reasonable compromise, monks being henceforth prohibited from preaching without the bishop's license in any churches but those of their own order. The question of residence was by the Pope's wish adjourned.

Thus the council, now augmented by Swiss and many other bishops, while all the chief Catholic powers except Poland were represented by ambassadors, could venture to approach those questions of dogma which the Emperor would gladly have seen postponed, so long as he was still pausing on the brink of his conflict with the German Protestants. The Pope, on the contrary, while ostentatiously displaying on the frontier the auxiliary forces which he had promised to the Emperor, was eager to proclaim through the council as distinctly as possible the solid unity of the orthodox Church. The doctrine concerning original sin having been promulgated in the teeth of imperial opposition, the legates pressed for the issue of the decree concerning justification. In the midst of the debates the Smalcaldic War broke out (July 1546).

For a time it seemed as if at Trent too the opposing interests would have proved irreconcileable. Pole, as the justification decree began to shape itself, had, "for reasons of health," withdrawn to Padua; Madruccio and Del Monte exchanged personal insults; Pacheco accused the legates of gross chicanery, and they in their turn threatened a removal of the council to an Italian city, where, in accordance with what they knew to be the

*Conflicts between the Imperialist and the Papal policy of the Council.*

Papal wish, the council might deliberate without being either overawed by the Emperor or menaced by his Protestant adversaries. Soon, however, the case was altered by the manifest collapse of the latter, notwithstanding their expectations of support from England, Denmark, and France, long before their final catastrophe in the battle of Mühlberg (April 24, 1547). The Emperor would not hear of the removal of the council to Lucca, Ferrara, or any other Italian town, and in consequence the plan of campaign at Trent was modified, in order at all events to make the breach with the Protestants impassable. The debates on justification were eagerly pushed on, and, after some further trials of *finesse*, the decree on the subject which anathematised the fundamental doctrines of the Lutheran Reformation was passed in the sixth session of the council (13th January 1547). On the other hand, the decree on residence was again postponed, and a very high tone was taken towards the prelates absent from the council—the German being, of course, those principally glanced at. In the next session (5th March) decrees followed asserting the orthodox doctrine of the Church concerning the sacraments, and baptism and confirmation in particular, and with these was at last issued the decree concerning residence. It avoided pronouncing on the view which had been so ardently advocated by the Spanish bishops and argued by the pen of Archbishop Carranza, that the duty of residence was imposed by divine law, and it took care to safeguard the dispensing authority of the Roman See. Yet, though at times evaded or overridden, the prohibition of pluralism contained in this decree, together with certain other provisions for the *bonâ fide* execution of bishops' functions, has indisputably proved most advantageous to the vigour and vitality of the episcopacy of the Church of Rome.

Paul III.'s attitude towards the Emperor had meanwhile grown more and more suspicious. Partly they had become antagonists on the great question of Church reorganisation; partly the Emperor was becoming disposed to thwart the dynastic policy of the Farnese; partly, again, the Pope now thought himself able to fall back on the alliance of France. In January Paul III. recalled the auxiliaries and stopped the subsidies which he had furnished to Charles V.; and in March Henry II. succeeded to the French throne, whose intrigues with the German Protestants, though leaving unaffected his fanatical rigour against his own heretics at home, seemed likely to break the current of imperial success. Thus at Trent the struggle against the Spanish bishops acquired an intense significance; and in the eighth session (11th March) the legates at last made use of the power entrusted to them, it was said, eighteen months before, and carried, against the votes of Spain, the removal of the council to Bologna, on the plea of an outbreak of the plague at Trent. By the Emperor's desire the Spanish bishops, plague or no plague, remained in the city.

<small>The removal to Bologna.</small>

'The obstinate old man,' said Charles, 'would end by ruining the Church;' and sanguine Protestants might dream of a renewal of the situation of 1526–27. The progress of events widened the breach between the Emperor and the Pope. After Mühlberg Charles V.

seemed irresistible, and as he would hear of no solution but a return of the council to Trent, there seemed no choice between submission and defiance. Gradually, however, it became clear that he had no wish again to drive things to extremes, and least of all to provoke anything of the nature of a schism. Moreover, France, where the Guises were now in the ascendant, was becoming more hostile to him; and the murder of the Pope's son at Piacenza, followed by the occupation of that city by Spanish troops (September 1547), nearly brought about the conclusion of a Franco-Italian league against Charles. But though French bishops arrived at Bologna, their attitude there was by no means acceptable to the Pope, and Henry II. had no real intention of making war upon the Emperor. Thus the latter thought himself able to take into his own hands the settlement of the religious difficulty. At the Diet of Augsburg, called 'the mailed diet,' because it was surrounded by the imperial soldiery, certain of the Protestant princes declared their readiness to submit to the council, while the Catholics demanded its removal back to Trent—a demand urged by the Emperor at both Bologna and Rome. But in the spring of 1548 came the worse news that the diet had passed the *Interim*, which, without sanction or cognisance of Rome, conceded to the Protestants the marriage of priests, the use of the cup by the laity, and a relaxation of the obligations of fasting. The *Interim*, it is true, was repudiated by the Catholic potentates, while the Protestants in many places had to be dragooned into accepting it; but the Emperor continued san-

*The Augsburg Interim.*

guine, published at the diet an edict announcing a series of Church reforms, and indulged a fancy that his offered compromise would tempt England and the Scandinavian North—peradventure even the intelligent Czar of Muscovy—back into the fold. At Rome, Paul took advantage of the consternation created by the Emperor's religious *coup d'état* to suggest a conference in the Papal city itself of bishops from both Trent and Bologna; but the proposal soon fell to the ground, and the *Interim* was referred to a congregation of cardinals, including Pole, appointed to report on the state of the Church. In the meantime, a commission of bishops was, at the Emperor's request, sent into Germany to superintend the working of the *Interim*—really to impede it, so far as might be. In the same month (September) the meetings of the so-called council at Bologna, where nothing had been accomplished, formally came to an end. The almost pathetic obstinacy of Charles in forcing through his *Interim* might have sufficed to warn the Pope of the uselessness of further resistance; but his anxiety about Parma and Piacenza probably contributed to make him give way. In the midst of further disappointments and of fresh designs, the immediate purposes of which are not altogether clear, Pope Paul III. died (15th November 1549). That the most generous of the aspirations which had under his reign first found full opportunity for asserting themselves had survived his manœuvring, was shown by the favourable reception, both outside and inside the conclave, of the proposal that Reginald Pole should be his successor. But Pole refused to be elected by the impulsive method of adoration, and in the end the Farnese interest, supported by the French, prevailed, and Cardinal del Monte was chosen.

The Papal government of Julius III. (1550–55) showed hardly more of temperate wisdom than had marked his conduct of the presidency at Trent; but he had the courage at the very outset to decide upon the safest course. The triumph of the House of Habsburg seemed complete; this was the period of the celebrated Family Compact (March 1551), which dealt with the succession to the Holy Roman Empire itself as with a chattel of the dynasty. At the diet held at Augsburg in 1550, the majority of the Protestant estates declared themselves ready to accept the *Interim*, and Maurice, now Elector of Saxony, proffered his services to force it on the unwilling. Regardless, therefore, of the overtures, and then of the menaces of France, Julius III. threw over the Farnese interest, and gave in his adhesion to the ecclesiastical policy of the Emperor. The friends of reform may have had their doubts as to the two commissions which he immediately instituted, the one (with Pole as a member) to amend the method of appointment to benefices, the other to improve the system of conclaves; but after a few conditions, most of them quite in the spirit of the imperial policy, had been proposed and accepted, the bull summoning the council to Trent for the following spring was issued without further ado (November).

*Paul III. succeeded by Julius III.*

Yet even before the council actually reopened (1st May 1551), it had become evident that the Papal view of its purposes remained as widely divergent from the Imperial as in the days of Paul III. The nomination of Cardinal Crescentio, a Roman by birth, as president of the council, with two Italian prelates, Pighino of Siponto and Lippomano of Verona, by his side, was in itself ominous; and the German Protestants, upon whom the Emperor pressed safe-conducts at Augsburg (1551), perceived the Papal intention of treating the Council as a mere continuation of that which had previously sat at Trent. Still, several of them, as well as the Catholic Electors, finally promised to attend. On the other hand Henry II. of France prohibited the appearance of a single French prelate, and began to talk of a Gallican council. Wroth with the Pope, and on the best of terms with heretic England, he was on the eve of forming an alliance with some of the Protestant princes of the Empire, fatal alike to its territorial integrity and to all schemes for the restoration of its religious unity (Alliance of Chambord, January 1552).

*Reopening of the Council at Trent.*

Thus the brief series of sessions held at Trent from May 1551 to April 1552 proved in the main, though not altogether, barren of results. While explicitly asserting the doctrine of transubstantiation, the council left open the *quomodo* of the Divine Presence, on which the Dominicans and the Franciscans were at issue not less than the Lutherans and the Calvinists; and though, to humour the Emperor, a decision on the permissibility of administration *sub utrâque* was adjourned, the majority of Spanish as well as of Italian bishops showed themselves averse to any concession on the subject. Nor could any one besides the Emperor found hopes upon the arrival of the ambassadors of certain Protestant princes (Brandenburg, Würtemberg, and some of the Free Towns), between whom and the council, notwithstanding certain courtesies, an attitude of defiance was virtually maintained. Unless the assembled fathers were prepared to reconsider the decrees already passed, and to force the assent of the Pope to a religious policy of quite unprecedented breadth, another deadlock was at hand; and already in the early months of 1552, the council, this time with the manifest connivance of Rome, began to thin. When, in April, Maurice of Saxony, now the ally of France, approached the southern frontier of the Empire, the Pope, whose own French war had taken a disastrous turn, had reason enough for shunning further co-operation with the Emperor. The council dwindled apace in spite of the efforts of Charles V., who had never ceased to believe in his schemes. Finally, however, he could not prevent the remnants of the council from passing a decree suspending its sessions for two years, which was opposed by not more than a dozen loyal Spanish votes (April 28, 1552). Cardinal Crescentio himself, whose Roman pride had not helped to render productive the second period of the council, was not present at its close, and died shortly afterwards. The possibility, if it had ever existed, of Western Christendom being reunited by the council on a basis corresponding to that of the imperial *Interim* had passed away to return no more; in its place, the Empire, in the Religious Peace of Augsburg (1555), acknowledged the dualism which rent it asunder, and accepted the principle, so far as Catholics and Lutherans were concerned, that each territorial authority in the Empire should, with certain modifications, determine which of

*The Council again suspended.*

the two creeds should be professed by its subjects. Thus Charles V.'s resignation of his thrones (1554–56) resulted, though far from being so intended, in a confession of his failure. While it was in progress, Julius III. died (23rd March 1555), leaving behind him scant evidence to support the rumour of his having indulged, at all events in the last period of his reign, in ideas of Church reformation. But the choice of his successor, Marcellus II. (April–May 1555), shows that these ideas were not yet extinct in the Sacred College, notwithstanding the simultaneous creation by Julius III. of fourteen cardinals; for Cervino had always been reckoned a member, though a moderate one, of the reforming party. Far greater, however, was the significance attaching to the election of the Pope who speedily took the place of Marcellus. The pontificate of Paul IV. (Gian Pietro Caraffa, May 1555–August 1559) forms one of the most remarkable chapters in the history of the Counter-Reformation, which in him seemed under both its aspects to have secured the mastery of the Church. God's will alone, he was convinced, had placed him where he stood; for he was unconscious of having achieved anything through the favour of man. He was now seventy-nine years of age, but he had never been more eager to devote himself to his chosen purpose,—the establishment in the eyes of all peoples of a pure and spiritually active Church, free from all impediments of corruptions and abuses, and purged of all poison of heresy and schism. Fully aware (though he had belonged to it himself) of the virtual failure of Paul III.'s commission of reform, Paul IV., who in his first bull had solemnly promised

*Pope Paul IV.*

an effectual reform of the Church and the Roman Curia, lost no time in instituting a congregation for the purpose. The commission, which consisted of three divisions, each of them composed jointly of cardinals, bishops, and doctors, wisely addressed itself in the first instance to the question of ecclesiastical appointments. The new Pope likewise issued orders for the specific reform of monastic establishments, and his energy seemed to stand in striking contrast with the hesitations and delays of the recently suspended council.

But once more the seductions of the temporal power overcame its holder. Caraffa's residence in Spain, and enthusiasm for the religious ideals and methods prevalent there, had not eradicated the bitterly anti-Spanish feeling inborn in him as a Neapolitan, and Charles V., returning hatred for hatred, had done his utmost to offend the dignity and damage the interests of the cardinal. To these personal and national sentiments had been added the conviction that the Emperor's dealings with the German Protestants had encouraged them to deal a deadly blow to the unity and strength of the Church; and thus Paul IV. allowed himself to be borne away by passion. His fiery temperament, fretted rather than soothed by old age, left him and those around him no peace; he maltreated the imperialist cardinals and the dependants of the Emperor within his reach, and sought to instigate the French Government to take up arms once more. Then, nothing would content his patriotic fury but the liberation of Italy from the presence of the foreigner. Taking advantage of a difference with Philip of Spain concerning the revocation of certain bulls concerning the Spanish Church and Inquisition, he directed a legal suit of excommunication to be instituted against Charles and Philip at Rome (1556). Intent solely upon the satisfaction of his passions, he raised to the purple, and soon intrusted with the main conduct of affairs, his nephew, Carlo Caraffa, a reckless soldier, full of grievances against the Emperor. His other nephews, when after a time they rallied to his anti-Spanish policy, he loaded with wealth and honours. In the war which ensued, but for the self-restraint of Alva, another sack of Rome might have been perpetrated by Spanish soldiery, and the quarrel pushed to an extreme issue; for the cardinal-nephew was already negotiating alliances with infidels and heretics. But the Spanish occupation of Naples was not to be shaken, and the great Spanish victory of St. Quentin (10th August 1557), put an end to all further hopes of French aid. When Rome was once more threatened by a Spanish army, the Pope was universally execrated as the source of all these ills. Fortunately for Paul IV., the judicious moderation of Spain gave him an undeserved opportunity of retreat; but though appearances were saved in the peace respectfully offered him by Alva (September 1557), the Spanish power stood fixed more firmly than ever in both the North and the South of Italy.

*The Marian reaction in England.*

The vehement political efforts of Paul IV., and their failure, could not in the end but damage the position of the Church in Italy. Elsewhere —in England—Spain and Rome were about this time supposed to be co-operating for the restoration of the orthodox faith. The people at large acquiesced in Queen Mary's measures, the majority perhaps with a comforting suspicion that her religion was, on the whole, from more than one point of view, the safer to prefer. At first, indeed, as Mary herself confessed to Pole, the mind of her people remained so strongly prepossessed against the Pope, that his supremacy was more difficult of acceptance to them than all the other tenets of her creed; but before long many were cured of their hesitation by the bull which Pole as Papal legate brought with him to England, confirming the possessors of monastery lands in their tenure. The impression created by the persecutions which ensued upon the formal reconciliation of England to Rome (30th November 1554) was probably neither so deep nor so widespread as has been frequently supposed. The real cause of Mary's unpopularity lay in the obstinacy with which she forced upon the nation first the Spanish marriage and then the Spanish policy. By the end of her reign the fruits of her infatuation were bitter as ashes in the mouths of Englishmen; so that when under Elizabeth, the doings of the Spanish Inquisition formed the staple of news brought home in ships, and when sentiments of patriotic indignation gathered round the nucleus of positive Protestant sentiment, strengthened by the return of religious refugees, the memories of Smithfield, Oxford, and Canterbury added very notably to the blaze of popular resentment. Thus public feeling, not less than the consistent counsels of her foremost statesmen, steadied Elizabeth's faltering hand; and under her England became Protestant, not indeed as yielding to any great wave of national opinion, but neither in mere passive obedience to a fresh series of statutes and ordinances. The disciplinary measures recommended by Pole, more especially at the synod held by him towards the close of 1555, bear a striking resemblance to some of the decrees passed at Trent in the first period of the council. His very acceptance of Canterbury he made conditional on residence. Manifestly the submission of the English Church to the Pope in Pole's eyes formed only half of his task. Here, as elsewhere, the Church must by reformation be brought nearer to his lofty ideal. But this it was not given to him to accomplish. As there is nothing to show that Paul IV. objected to the proceedings of Pole in England, his recall (subsequently modified in form rather than in substance) might be regarded as part of the Pope's general policy of offence against Spain, were it not for apprehensions of Caraffa's ill-will towards him, avowed by Pole before the elevation of the former to the Papacy. In any case, Pole's death (18th November 1558), which followed that of Charles V. within less than two months, seems to close a distinct page in the history of the Counter-Reformation. A politic assumption of confidence on the part of the Pope towards Queen Mary's successor might perhaps have delayed the re-emancipation of the Church of England, and thus also have retarded the complete victory of a more advanced type of Protestantism on the other side of the Border. But Paul IV. dreaded no step which Elizabeth could take so much as her marriage with Philip of Spain. It was the same hatred and fear of Habsburg which led him to drive the new Emperor Ferdinand I. halfway into the arms of the German Protestants, or at least into a system

*Death of Cardinal Pole.*

of government by compromise irreconcilable with the principles upheld at Rome.

In the states of the Church, however, and within the range of his Italian influence, time was still left to Paul IV. for the assertion of these principles; nor is there anything more extraordinary in his life than the exertions of the last two years of his reign. At first it seemed as if he would need some time to steady himself after the collapse of his political schemes, and as if he were unprepared to adopt Cardinal Pacheco's outspoken advice and let reform begin at home. But of a sudden, as if in another gust of passion, he made a clean sweep of the obstacles which his own perversity had placed in his path; banished his nephews, changed his whole administration, and then took up in terrible earnest the work of Church reform. He would allow no appointment savouring of corruption to any spiritual office; he would hear of no exception to the duty of residence; he completely abolished dispensations for marriages within prohibited degrees. Into the general management of the churches of the city, as well as into that of his own Papal court, he introduced so strict a discipline that Rome was likened to a well-conducted monastery. But the agency which above all others he encouraged was that which his own advice had established in the centre of the Catholic world,—the Inquisition. From the Sacred College downwards (as in the case of Cardinal Morone), no sphere of life was exempted from its control; and his intolerance extended itself to the very Jews, whose privileges in the Papal states he ruthlessly revoked. On his deathbed he

*Paul IV. and the Counter-Reformation.*

recommended the Inquisition with the Holy See itself to the pious cardinals surrounding him. It was afterwards observed that many reforms decreed in its third period by the Council of Trent were copied from the ordinances issued by Paul IV. in this memorable *biennium*. But inasmuch as during his Pontificate the Church of Rome had lost ground in almost every country of Europe except Italy and Spain, his death (18th August 1559) naturally brought with it a widespread renewal of the demand for remedies more effective than those supplied by his feverish activity and by the operations of his favourite institution.

Personally, Pius IV. (1559-66) was regarded, and probably chosen, as an opponent of the late Pope; his family history inclined him to the imperial interest, and he was understood to favour concessions to Germany with a view of bringing her stray sheep back into the fold. He possessed, with a genial disposition, a reasonable mind; and though an excellent canon lawyer, was far too little of a theologian to love dwelling in extremes of dogma. He showed no disposition to follow his predecessor in prohibiting the sale of spiritual dignities, benefices, and favours of all kinds; but in general he furthered rather than arrested the religious reaction. Above all, the Inquisition, though he is not known to have done anything to intensify its rigour or augment its authority, went on as before. For himself, he avoided the nepotism of which, in the pursuit of his political ends, Paul IV. had made himself guilty. In contrast with the Caraffa nephews, on whom he allowed a terrible vengeance to descend, Carlo Borromeo, the nephew of Pius

IV., served the Holy See in a spirit of unselfish devotion, and began those efforts on behalf of religion which in the end obtained for him a place among the saints of the Church,—a position not reached by many Pope's nephews. With the aid of this influence, Pius IV. came to perceive that the future, both of the Church and of the Papacy, depended on the spirit of confidence and cohesion which could be infused into the former; nor had he from the very outset of his pontificate ever doubted the expediency of reassembling the council at Trent.

The Emperor Ferdinand and the French government, who still persisted in treating the reunion of the Church as the primary object of the council, at first strongly urged the substitution for Trent of a genuinely German or French town, where the German bishops, and perhaps even the Protestants, would feel no scruple about attending. But a totally free and *new* council of this description lay outside the horizon of the Papacy; and Pius IV. might have let fall the plan altogether, but for the fear of the entire separation in that event of the Gallican Church from Rome. In France Protestantism had made considerable strides during the reign of Henry II. (1547-59), more especially of late under cover of the war with Spain, although that war advanced the influence of the Guises, represented in the Church by the Cardinal of Lorraine. The introduction of the Inquisition (1557) had remained a futile attempt; and though after the peace of Câteau-Cambrésis Henry II. actually proposed to Philip a joint attack upon Geneva, Protestantism flourished, especi-

*The religious condition of France.*

ally in the south and west of the monarchy, in spite of persecution; and about six weeks before the death of Henry II. the first national synod of Protestants was held at Paris (May 1559). Under Francis II. the Guise influence became paramount, the persecution of the Protestants continued, and was expedited by the edict of Romorantin (May 1560). But though the suppression, just before this, of the so-called conspiracy of Amboise had temporarily added to the power of the Guises, it had also made the Queen Mother, Catharine de' Medici, resolve not to let the power of the state pass wholly out of her hands. Hence the appointment of the large-hearted L'Hôpital as chancellor, and the Assembly of Notables at Fontainebleau (August), where the grievances against Rome found full expression, and where arrangements were made for a meeting of the States-General and a national council of the French Church. This resolution determined Pius IV. to lose no further time. He succeeded in overcoming the objections of both Ferdinand and the French Government to Trent, and adjourned the more difficult question as to whether the new assembly should or should not be regarded as a mere continuation of the former, which France had never acknowledged. On 29th November 1560 he issued a bull summoning all the prelates and princes of Christendom to Trent for the following Easter. The invitation included both Eastern schismatics and Western heretics, Elizabeth of England among the rest; but neither she nor the German Protestant princes assembled at Naumburg, nor the kings of the Scandinavian North, would so much as receive the

Papal summons. In France, the death of Francis II. (5th December 1560) further depressed the Guise influence; and Catharine entered into negotiations with the Pope with a view to concessions such as would satisfy the Huguenots while approved by the French bishops. She considerably raised her demands not long before the Colloquy of Poissy, (September 1561), which, however, notwithstanding its array of ecclesiastical notabilities on both sides, came to nothing, owing in part to the active intrigues of the Papal nuncio. But the 'Edict of January' (1562), which followed, long remained a sort of standard of fair concessions to the Huguenots.

Under these circumstances there was little prospect of France being for some time to come represented at Trent except by ambassadors with instructions very unacceptable to the Papal policy. From the Empire, too, neither Catholic nor Protestant princes could be prevailed upon to attend; and a commission appointed by Ferdinand carried its demands for ecclesiastical reforms so far (September 1561) that he had to moderate their tone before incorporating them in his *Libellus de reformatione*, afterwards presented to the council. Even King Sebastian of Portugal about this time formulated a series of very substantial articles of reformation for presentation at Trent. Philip II. of Spain completely approved of this proceeding, and supported the demand of the other powers for a free council. At the same time, however, both he and the Spanish bishops were resolved to maintain the rigid standard of doctrine proclaimed in the earlier sessions of the council, and to allow no concessions to Protestant

*Re-opening of the Council of Trent.*

claims or sympathies. Thus, after all, the new assembly was not likely to be altogether unmanageable; and Pius IV. took care to keep up the numbers of the Italian bishops, besides appointing not less than five legates to conduct the proceedings. These legates were mostly moderate men. Such was pre-eminently the character of Hercules Gonzaga, cardinal of Mantua, the presiding legate, a *persona gratissima* to the Emperor. With him, Cardinal Puteo, an accomplished canonist, had been originally named, but he was disabled by illness just before the meeting of the council. The others were Cardinals Seripando, formerly general of the Augustines, and now archbishop of Salerno, a learned and moderate-minded prelate; Simonetta, whom Sadolet extols as unanimously acknowledged to be the greatest lawyer of the age; and Cardinal Hosius, afterwards the principal figure in the Polish Counter-Reformation. He was probably selected as having for some time held the nunciature at the Emperor's court, and being well acquainted with his views. Simonetta seems to have been regarded as the representative proper of the Papal policy. For Puteo was afterwards substituted the Cardinal of Hohenems (Altemps), bishop of Constance, a young nephew of the Pope. Soon after the re-opening of the council Pius IV. characteristically directed another relative, the able Bishop of Ventimiglia (Visconti), to watch the proceedings of the two senior legates, who with their colleagues seem in their turn to have employed the same agent to watch the conduct of the Cardinal of Lorraine.

Was the council which held its first public session on 18th January 1562 to be regarded as a new council, or as a continuation of that which had previously sat in the same locality? This was no merely theoretical question, for on the answer would depend two issues inseparable from one another. In the first place, would the new assembly resume the labours of the previous one at the point they had reached, more especially in the enunciation of true Catholic doctrine? and, again, would it refuse to reopen the door deliberately shut by its predecessor upon a policy which aimed at reconciling the Protestants to the Church? To ensure affirmative answers to both these questions was naturally the desire both of Rome and of the Spanish bishops, and those who were, like them, intent upon the establishment of a vigorous Church discipline rooted in a strong episcopacy, but, above all, upon the definitive declaration of a rigid body of Catholic doctrine. The opposite view was, however, long favoured by the Emperor Ferdinand, supported by a public sentiment practically universal in the Empire, and by France, where bigotry and faction had not yet quenched the national desire for ecclesiastical independence and political unity. Not very dissimilar were the issues turning on the further question as to the acceptance of the new principle of conducting the business of the council. This principle, which the legates sought to introduce by a procedure the reverse of straightforward, reserved to themselves the initiative of proposing subjects of discussion to the council. Vehemently resisted by some of the Spanish bishops, the formula was maintained, even after Philip II. had sought the assistance of the Emperor and the kings of France and Portugal for

*Proponentibus legatis.*

bringing about its removal, and after Pius IV. had himself agreed to concede the point. Thus the council was, down to its close, very effectively prevented from enlarging the scope of its proceedings at the risk of interfering with their deliberately designed plan. For, though amidst many vexatious delays, at the last preceded by all but reckless haste, the original plan of the council was actually carried out, and this with a degree of success of which it is futile to lose sight because of the intrigues and manœuvres, and the struggle of interests and passions, obscuring it in the pages of partisan historians.

In this concluding period the Italian bishops preponderated more than ever; next to them the Spaniards were again the most numerous; but though, as a body, still faithful to their programme, both on questions of doctrine where they agreed with the Papal party, and on questions of discipline where they differed from it, they no longer voted as a solid phalanx, and their leader, Archbishop Guerrero of Granada, commanded no unbroken allegiance. Moreover, the Jesuit Salmeron, who discharged the duties of Papal theologian, and a little later the Jesuit general Lainez, who bore himself as the intellectual master of the assembly, represented an element in the religious life of Spain which claimed attention in spite of either bishops or king. No prelates attended either from the Empire at large or from Poland, the proxies whom they sent being naturally enough refused a hearing by the majority. Hungary and Bohemia were represented by a few bishops. The French prelates, with the Cardinal of Lorraine at their head, did not arrive

*Composition of the Council.*

till late in the day (November 1562). Thus the opposition to the Papal management of the council was during the greater part of this year conducted by a co-operation between the imperial and French ambassadors, occasionally productive of brave words, but ineffectual in its final results.

The first deliberations of the reassembled council were barren, for the definitive adoption of the index of prohibited books was deferred to the close of the council, when it was, after all, handed over to the Pope; and though a safe-conduct was granted to Protestants desirous of attending at Trent, no Protestant government or prelates availed themselves of it, while the heretical subjects of Catholic states were expressly excluded from its use. Hereupon, however, the council attempted again to proceed *pari passu* with dogma and discipline. On the latter head in particular, the imperial and the French ambassadors at different times presented very distinct demands, in the so-called 'libels of reformation' laid by them before the council; but in neither case were these programmes seriously taken up. One disciplinary question of paramount importance might, however, have speedily been carried to a satisfactory issue, could the manifest advantage of the Church have prevailed over the baser interests of the Roman Court. This was the question of residence and of its divine origin, as constituting an obligation upon bishops and priests charged with a cure of souls. On this head a complete agreement existed between the Governments and the episcopal party, and the Pope himself was known to have declared to the cardinals at Rome his conviction

*Principal questions at issue.*

of the divine origin of the duty. Thus two of the legates (Gonzaga and Seripando) were prepared to give way to 'ultramontane' opinion on the subject, though Simonetta unfalteringly upheld the Roman view. When (April 1562) they actually put the question to the vote, nearly half the assembly affirmed the divine origin, while about a quarter voted in the negative, and another quarter (or slightly more) for referring the matter to the Pope. Hereupon the latter changed his attitude, and when the question, which had seemed shelved, was once more revived, threatened to dismiss the presiding legate for sacrificing the welfare of the Holy See. But though he for a time talked of removing the council once more to an Italian city, Pius IV. had no real reason for fearing a dangerous show of independence at Trent, and Philip II. himself gave orders that the question of residence should for the present be allowed to slumber. In the meantime another struggle had begun in connexion with the formulation of the dogmatic decrees concerning the sacraments, on the subject of the concession of the cup to the laity. This, the chief concession made to the German Protestants in the *Interim* of 1548, was demanded both in the imperial and in the French *libel;* and it was known to be viewed without disfavour by the Pope himself, whose predecessor, Paul III., had formerly, at the request of Charles V., empowered a commission of bishops to accord it to individual claimants in the Empire. The denial of the Cup to the laity was a relatively modern practice in the Western Church, and its use was accordingly now, as it had been at Basel, a mere question of expediency.

The Spanish episcopate, however, herein thoroughly in harmony with Philip II., would listen to no such proposals, while in the eyes of the Papal party—more Papal than the Pope, and encouraged in its persistency by the ruthless oratory of Lainez—to yield on one head seemed the preface to yielding on all. When the vote was taken (September 1562), only 48 were found ready to allow the concession of the cup—some to the laity of the Empire and its dependencies, some to that of Hungary and Bohemia only,—while 52, with or without qualifications, refused the proposal, and 65 relegated the matter to the decision of the Pope. Not many days afterwards, a previous effort in the same direction having failed, this course was finally agreed upon by an overwhelming majority, composed of members voting from very different points of view.

The question which really came home to the fathers of the Church assembled at Trent presented itself again when the sacrament of orders had in due course to be debated. The imperial and French ambassadors still co-operated as actively as ever, and the episcopal party, the Spanish prelates in particular, entered upon the struggle with a full sense of its critical importance. If the right divine of episcopacy could be declared, with it would be established the divine obligation of residence. Pius IV. accordingly showed considerable shrewdness in instructing the legates at once to formulate a decree on residence, which, while leaving the question of divine obligation open, imposed penalties on non-residence (except for lawful reasons), sufficient to meet practical requirements. But though such a decree was passed by the council, the debates on the origin of the episcopal office, which involved nothing less than the origin and nature of the Papal supremacy, continued (November); and the critical nature of the discussion was the more apparent when in the midst of it there at last arrived nearly a score of French bishops, headed by the Cardinal of Lorraine. Hitherto France had been represented at the council by spokesmen of the French court and of the Parliament of Paris; now, the foremost among the prelates of the monarchy, whose abilities, however, unfortunately fell far short of his pretensions, announced in full conciliar assembly the demands of his branch of the Church. The recent January edict proved the strength of the Huguenots in France; and though the Cardinal's first speech at Trent breathed nothing but condemnation of these heretics, it suited him to pose as the advocate of as extensive a series of reforms as had yet been urged upon the council. Further additions were made in the 'libel' already mentioned, which was shortly afterwards (January 1563) presented by the French ambassador, and perfect harmony existed between the French and the imperial policy at the council. What decision, then, was to be expected on the crucial question as to the relations between Papal and episcopal authority? How could a recognition of the Pope's claim to be regarded as *rector universalis ecclesiæ* be expected from such a union of the ultramontane forces? The current was not likely to be stopped by the provisions for checking some of the abuses of the Papal court, which about this time Pius IV. announced on his own account at Rome; it seemed on the point of rising higher than ever when (February 1563) the Cardinal of Lorraine and some other prelates waited upon the Emperor at Innsbruck. In truth, however, a turning-point in the history of the council was close at hand.

The Cardinal of Lorraine had left Trent for Innsbruck with threats of a Gallican synod on his lips. Ferdinand I. had arrived there very wroth with the council, and had received the Bishop of Zante (Commendone), whom the legates sent to deprecate his vexation, with marked coolness. The remedies proposed to the Emperor by the Cardinal were drastic enough; the council was to be swamped by French, German, and Spanish bishops, and the Emperor, by repairing to Trent in person, was to awe the assembly into discussing the desired reforms, whether with or without the approval of the legates. But Ferdinand I., by nature moderate in action, and taught by the example of his brother, Charles V., the danger of violent courses, preferred to resort to a series of direct and by no means tame appeals to the Pope. The latter, indisposed as he was to support a fresh proposition for the removal of the council to some German town, urged by France but resisted by Spain, which at the same time persistently opposed the concession of the cup demanded by both France and the Emperor, saw his opportunity for taking his adversaries singly. The deaths about this time (March 1563) of the presiding legate, Cardinal Gonzaga, and of his colleague Cardinal Seripando, both of whom had occasionally shown themselves inclined to yield to the reforming party, were likewise in his favour. Their places were filled by Cardinals Morone, formerly a prisoner indicted by the Inquisition, now an eager

*Ferdinand I. gained over to the Papal policy.*

champion of Papal claims, and Navagero, a Venetian by birth, but not in his political sentiments. Morone, though he had left Rome almost despairing of any favourable issue of the council, at once began to negotiate with the Emperor through the Jesuit Canisius. The leverage employed may, in addition to the distrust between Ferdinand and his Spanish nephew, and the ancient jealousy between Austria and France, have included some reference to the heterodox opinions and the consequently doubtful prospects of the Emperor's eldest son, Maximilian. In a word, the Papal government about this time formed and carried out a definite plan for inducing the Emperor to abandon his conciliar policy. The consideration offered for his assenting to a speedy termination of the council was the promise that, so soon as that event should have taken place, the desired concession of the cup should be made to his subjects. Ferdinand I., without becoming a thoroughgoing partisan of the Papal policy, accepted the bargain as seemingly the shortest road to the end which, for the sake of the peace of the Empire, he had at heart. Thus, notwithstanding the continued opposition of the French bishops, the decrees concerning the episcopate began to shape themselves more easily, and the Pope of his own accord submitted to the council certain canons of a stringent kind, reforming in a similar way the discipline of the cardinalate (June). And when, in the course of a violent quarrel about precedence between the kings of France and Spain, the latter, enraged at his demands not being enforced by the Pope, had threatened by insisting on the admission of Protestants to the council indefinitely to prolong it, the Emperor intervened against the proposal. But the conflict between the Papal and the episcopal authority seemed still incapable of solution, and though Lainez audaciously demanded the reference of all questions of reform to the sole decision of the Pope, and denounced the opposition of the French bishops as proceeding from members of a schismatic Church, this opposition steadily continued in conjunction with that of the Spaniards, and still found a leader in the Cardinal of Lorraine.

Yet at this very time a change began to be perceptible in the conduct of this versatile and ambitious prelate. The Cardinal was supposed to have himself aspired to the office of presiding legate, and though he had missed this place of honour and power, the condition of things in France was such as naturally to incline him in the direction of Rome. The assassination of his brother Francis, Duke of Guise (February 1563), deprived his family and interest of their natural chief, and inclined Catharine de' Medici to transact with the Huguenots. The Cardinal accordingly became anxious at the same time to return to France and prevent the total eclipse of the influence he had hitherto exercised at court, and to secure himself by an understanding with the Pope. A letter which about this time arrived from Mary Queen of Scots, declaring her readiness to submit to the decrees of the council, and, should she ascend the throne of England, to reduce that country to obedience to the Holy See, may perhaps be connected with these overtures. Pius IV., delighted to meet the Cardinal half-way, sent instructions in this

*The Cardinal of Lorraine gained over.*

sense to the legates, whom the recent display of Spanish arrogance had already disposed favourably towards France. Thus the decree on the sacrament of orders was passed in the colourless condition desired by the Papal party, in a session held on July 15, the Spanish bishops angrily declaring themselves betrayed by the French cardinal. Other decrees were passed in this memorable session, among them one of substantial importance for the establishment of diocesan seminaries for priests. Clearly, the council had now become tractable, and might speedily be brought to an end. In this sense the Pope addressed urgent letters to the three great Catholic monarchs, and found willing listeners, except in Spain.

Meanwhile the remaining decrees, both of doctrine and of discipline, were eagerly pushed on. The sacrament of marriage gave rise to much discussion; but the proposal that the marriage of priests should be permitted, though formerly included in both the imperial and the French libel, was now advocated only by the two prelates who spoke directly in the name of the Emperor. But in the decree proposed on the all-important subject of the reformation of the life and morals of the clergy, the legates presumed too far on the yielding mood of the governments. It not only contained many admirable reforms as to the conditions under which spiritual offices, from the cardinalate downwards, were to be held or conferred, but the Papacy had wisely and generously surrendered many existing usages profitable to itself. At the same time, however, it was proposed not only to deprive the royal authority

*The business of the Council wound up.*

in the several states of a series of analogous profits, but to take away from it the nomination of bishops and the right of citing ecclesiastics before a secular tribunal. To the protest which the ambassadors of the powers inevitably raised against these proposals, the legates replied by raising a cry that the "reformation of the princes" should be comprehended in the decrees. It became necessary to postpone the objectionable article; but now the fears of the supporters of the existing system began to be excited, both at Rome and at Trent, and it was contrived to introduce so many modifications into the proposed decree as seriously to impair its value. Then, though the Cardinal of Lorraine himself, during a visit to Rome (September), showed his readiness to support the Papal policy, the French ambassadors at the council carried their opposition to its encroachments upon the claims of their sovereign so far as to withdraw to Venice. And above all, the Spanish bishops, upheld by the persistency of their king, stood firmly by the original form of the reformation decree, and finally obtained its restoration to a very considerable extent. Thus the greater portion of the decree was at last passed in the penultimate session of the council (11th November).

With the exception of Spain, all the powers now made known their consent to winding up the business of the council without further loss of time. But Count Luna still immovably resisted the closing of the council before the express assent of King Philip should have been received; nor was it till the news—authentic or not

*Closing of the Council.*

—arrived of a serious illness having befallen the Pope that the fear of the complications which might arise in the event of his death put an end to further delay. Summoned in all haste, the fathers met on December 3rd for their five-and-twentieth session, and on this and the following day rapidly discussed a series of decrees, some of which were by no means devoid of intrinsic importance. In the doctrinal decrees concerning purgatory and indulgences, as in those concerning the invocation of saints and the respect due to their relics and images, it was sought to preclude a reckless exaggeration or distortion of the doctrines of the Church on these heads, and a corrupt perversion of the usages connected with them. (Thus the abuse of the so-called 'privileged altars' was not revived till the papacy of Gregory XIII.) Of the disciplinary decrees, the most important and elaborate related to the religious of both sexes. It contained a clause, inserted on the motion of Lainez, which the Jesuits afterwards interpreted as generally exempting their Society from the operation of this decree. Another decree enjoined sobriety and moderation in the use of the ecclesiastical penalty of excommunication. For the rest, all possible expedition was used in gathering up the threads of the work done or attempted by the council. The determination of the Index, as well as the revision of missal, breviary, ritual, and catechism, were remitted to the Pope. Then the decrees debated in the last session and at its adjourned meeting were adopted, being subscribed by 234 (or 255 ?) ecclesiastics; and the decrees passed in the sessions of the council before its re-assembling under Pope Pius IV. were read over again, and thus its continuity (1545—63) was established without any use being made of the terms 'approbation' and 'confirmation.' A decree followed, composed by the Cardinal of Lorraine and Cardinal Madruccio, solemnly commending the ordinances of the council to the Church and to the princes of Christendom, and remitting any difficulties concerning the execution of the decrees to the Pope, who would provide for it either by summoning another General Council or as he might determine. A concluding decree put an end to the council itself, which closed with a kind of general thanksgiving intoned by the Cardinal of Lorraine.

The decrees of the council were shortly afterwards (26th January 1564) ratified by Pius IV., against the wish of the more determined Curialists, while others would have wished him to guard himself by certain restrictions. These were, however, unnecessary, as he reserved to himself the interpretation of doubtful or disputed decrees. This reservation remained absolute as to decrees concerning dogma;[1] for the interpretation of those concerning discipline, Sixtus V. afterwards appointed a special commission under the name of the Congregation of the Council of Trent. While the former became *ipso facto* binding on the

*Reception of its decrees.*

---

[1] The *Catechismus Romanus*, drawn up by a commission of cardinals, and published by direction of Pius IV. (1566), cannot claim an authority equal to that of the *Canones et decreta Concilii Tridentini* (Rome, 1564). The catechisms composed by Canisius (1554 and 1566), though not sanctioned by the Pope, enjoyed a more widespread popular acceptance than the *Catechismus Romanus*.

C. H.   G

—arrived of a serious illness having befallen the Pope that the fear of the complications which might arise in the event of his death put an end to further delay. Summoned in all haste, the fathers met on December 3rd for their five-and-twentieth session, and on this and the following day rapidly discussed a series of decrees, some of which were by no means devoid of intrinsic importance. In the doctrinal decrees concerning purgatory and indulgences, as in those concerning the invocation of saints and the respect due to their relics and images, it was sought to preclude a reckless exaggeration or distortion of the doctrines of the Church on these heads, and a corrupt perversion of the usages connected with them. (Thus the abuse of the so-called 'privileged altars' was not revived till the papacy of Gregory XIII.) Of the disciplinary decrees, the most important and elaborate related to the religious of both sexes. It contained a clause, inserted on the motion of Lainez, which the Jesuits afterwards interpreted as generally exempting their Society from the operation of this decree. Another decree enjoined sobriety and moderation in the use of the ecclesiastical penalty of excommunication. For the rest, all possible expedition was used in gathering up the threads of the work done or attempted by the council. The determination of the Index, as well as the revision of missal, breviary, ritual, and catechism, were remitted to the Pope. Then the decrees debated in the last session and at its adjourned meeting were adopted, being subscribed by 234 (or 255?) ecclesiastics; and the decrees passed in the sessions of the council before its re-assembling under Pope Pius IV. were read over again, and thus its continuity (1545–63) was established without any use being made of the terms 'approbation' and 'confirmation.' A decree followed, composed by the Cardinal of Lorraine and Cardinal Madruccio, solemnly commending the ordinances of the council to the Church and to the princes of Christendom, and remitting any difficulties concerning the execution of the decrees to the Pope, who would provide for it either by summoning another General Council or as he might determine. A concluding decree put an end to the council itself, which closed with a kind of general thanksgiving intoned by the Cardinal of Lorraine.

The decrees of the council were shortly afterwards (26th January 1564) ratified by Pius IV., against the wish of the more determined Curialists, while others would have wished him to guard himself by certain restrictions. These were, however, unnecessary, as he reserved to himself the interpretation of doubtful or disputed decrees. This reservation remained absolute as to decrees concerning dogma;[1] for the interpretation of those concerning discipline, Sixtus V. afterwards appointed a special commission under the name of the Congregation of the Council of Trent. While the former became *ipso facto* binding on the

*Reception of its decrees.*

---

[1] The *Catechismus Romanus*, drawn up by a commission of cardinals, and published by direction of Pius IV. (1566), cannot claim an authority equal to that of the *Canones et decreta Concilii Tridentini* (Rome, 1564). The catechisms composed by Canisius (1554 and 1566), though not sanctioned by the Pope, enjoyed a more widespread popular acceptance than the *Catechismus Romanus*.

entire Church, the decrees on discipline and reformation could not become valid in any particular state till after they had been published in it with the consent of its government. This distinction is of the greatest importance. The doctrinal system of the Church of Rome was now enduringly fixed; the area which the Church had lost she could henceforth only recover if she reconquered it. Many attempts at reunion by compromise have since been made from the Protestant side, and some of these have perhaps been met half-way by the generous wishes of not a few Catholics; but the Council of Trent has doomed all these projects to inevitable sterility. The gain of the Church of Rome from her acquisition at Trent of a clearly and sharply defined 'body of doctrine' is not open to dispute, except from a point of view which her doctors have steadily repudiated. And it is difficult to suppose but that, in her conflict with the spirit of criticism which from the first in some measure animated the Protestant Reformation and afterwards urged it far beyond its original scope, the Church of Rome must have proved an unequal combatant, had not the Council of Trent renewed the foundations of the authority claimed by herself and of that claimed by her head on earth.

The effect of the disciplinary decrees of the council, though more far-reaching and enduring than has been on all sides acknowledged, was necessarily in the first instance dependent on the reception given to them by the several Catholic powers. The representatives of the Emperor at once signed the whole of the decrees of the council, though only on behalf of his hereditary dominions; and he had his promised reward when, a few months afterwards (April), the German bishops were, under certain restrictions, empowered to accord the cup in the Eucharist to the laity. But neither the Empire through its diet, nor Hungary, ever accepted the Tridentine decrees, though several of the Catholic estates of the Empire, both spiritual and temporal, individually accepted them with modifications. The example of Ferdinand was followed by several other Powers; but in Poland, the diet, to which the decrees were twice (1564 and 1578) presented as having been accepted by King Sigismund Augustus, refused to accord its own acceptance, maintaining that the Polish Church, as such, had never been represented at the council. In Portugal and in the Swiss Catholic cantons, the decrees were received without hesitation, as also by the Seigniory of Venice, whose representatives at Trent had rarely departed from an attitude of studied moderation, and who now merely safeguarded the rights of the Republic. True to the part recently played by him, the Cardinal of Lorraine, on his own responsibility, subscribed to the decrees in the name of the King of France. But the Parliament of Paris was on the alert, and on his return home the Cardinal had to withdraw in disgrace to Rheims. Neither the doctrinal decrees of the council nor the disciplinary, which in part clashed with the customs of the kingdom and the privileges of the Gallican Church, were ever published in France. The ambassador of Spain, whose king and prelates had so consistently held out against the closing of the council, refused his signature till he had received express instructions. Yet as it was Spain which had hoped and toiled for the achievement at the council of solid results, so it was here that the decrees fell on the most grateful soil, when, after considerable deliberation and delay, their publication at last took place, accompanied by stringent safeguards as to the rights of the king and the usages of his subjects (1565). The same course was adopted in the Italian and Flemish dependencies of the Spanish monarchy.

The disciplinary decrees of the council, on the whole, fell short in completeness of the doctrinal.

*Results.* But while they consistently maintained the Papal authority and confirmed its formal pretensions, the episcopal authority too was strengthened by them, not only as against the monastic orders, but in its own moral foundations. More than this, the whole priesthood, from the Pope downwards, benefited by the warnings that had been administered, by the sacrifices that had been made, and by the reforms that had been agreed upon. The Church became more united, less worldly, and more dependent on herself. These results outlasted the movement known as the Counter-Reformation, and should be ignored by no candid mind.

# CHAPTER IV.

## *THE COUNTER-REFORMATION AT ITS HEIGHT.*

THE period during which the movement of the Counter-Reformation arrived and maintained itself at its height may be reckoned as covering the thirty years or thereabouts that ensued upon the close of the Council of Trent. This period coincides with the main course of the great attempt of Philip II. of Spain to extinguish Protestantism in Europe. During these years, the few advances still made by Protestantism were more than counterbalanced by its losses elsewhere, while the Catholic reaction, on the other hand, fully developed its resources. It had now become an integral part of the ecclesiastical policy of Rome, which during far the greater portion of this period closely followed that of Spain, and never so much as contemplated a return to less direct and active courses.

*The religious policy of Philip II.*

From Spain, then, the entire movement, as before and at the Council of Trent, so during the preceding generation, received its chief impulses. The absolutism of the new Spanish monarchy enabled the will of Philip II. to reflect itself in the whole character of his government at home, and of its action and influence abroad. Whether or not he had momentarily winked at Protestantism in England, in his own kingdom he was the uncompromising champion of orthodoxy. His jealousy of his royal prerogatives, although it led to many troublesome differences between him and the Holy See, did not interfere with his fidelity to its interests and those of the Church. What he demanded was that even the Pope should only exercise power in Spain through and by means of him, the king. Of his European policy, which involved him in so much combative intrigue and aggressive war, the objects were no doubt largely fixed for him by the mere geographical conditions of his inheritance; but though these may have been the original causes of the chief contests of his reign, religious enthusiasm sustained the resolution of Philip in both instances, as it sped the galleons of the great Armada to their doom, and bound the arms of the Leaguers with the Castilian red.

The ecclesiastical agency on which Philip's system of government above all depended was that of the Inquisition, which had not only altogether subjugated the Spanish nation, but did its utmost, as cases like those of Luis de Leon (1571–76) and Archbishop Carranza show, to terrorise over the Spanish Church. At the same time it persecuted with unabated zeal whatever unusual efforts of learning and scholarship provoked suspicion, such as those of Francisco de Sanchez (El Brocense), the learned editor of early national poetry (1582). Moreover, the prohibitions of the Index were rigorously enforced by Philip, the penalties of confiscation of property, and even of

*Philip II. and the Inquisition.*

death, being denounced against those who infringed them. Popular feeling, no doubt, continued to meet this system of repression more than half-way. The Lutheran Reformation, if it had penetrated into Spain at all, had left no traces behind it; the Scriptures remained virtually unknown; nor is the absence of independent theological speculation disproved by such exceptions as that of the Navarrese Servetus. The universities were falling into decay. Alcala appealed to the Pope against Salamanca (1574), and Salamanca dwindled to half its former number of students, though an early edict of Philip II. (1558) had prohibited his subjects from resorting to foreign seats of learning. Inasmuch as the same condition of intellectual subjection prevailed in the reign of Philip III. (1598–1621), its impress is perceptible during a long period even in those branches of literature which might seem farthest removed from theology and moral philosophy. Thus the Spanish theatre was subjected to a rigorous censorship (1587), and would have come to an end through the fiat of the dying Philip II. (1598), were it as easy to suppress as it is to control the established amusements of a people.

But though the co-operation of the monarchy and the Inquisition could effect much, it could not sustain the spiritual enthusiasm to which, as a Spanish movement, the Counter-Reformation owed its origin. In a revival or uprising of this description, ideas must find personal representatives capable of satisfying the imagination of the people; and such were, in this period, the leading figures among the Spanish mystics, to the

*The spiritual influence of Spanish mysticism.*

earlier of whom reference has already been made. Such, above all, was the holy woman whom the national assembly of Spain saluted as a saint before she was canonised by Rome (1622), and whom many generations after her death insurgent patriotism named *generalissima* of the armies of Spain. The chief historical significance of the reformatory movement begun by St. Teresa after all lies in its having in a large measure met the religious aspirations of the national mind, thus occupying the ground elsewhere seized by dogmatic dissent or sectarianism. Teresa de Ahumada, or, as she afterwards called herself, Teresa de Jesus (1515–82), was of ancient Castilian lineage, and brought up to a love of chivalrous romance. She ran away to become a nun, but soon found the inside of the convent walls almost as worldly as the world without. Long years of poignant spiritual sufferings taught her the power and the rapture of prayer, and transformed without unhinging her mind. Towards the end of this period her Jesuit confessor and other members of his Society settled in her native town of Avila, encouraged her aspirations, and accepted her accounts of her visions. Yet the fire of action was after all kindled in her by the earlier example of St. Peter of Alcantara, whose bare-footed friars certainly suggested the foundation of the house of the discalced Carmelite nuns at Avila (1562), the beginning of a reform which, before Teresa's death, extended over seventy-three, and within about two centuries over more than seven hundred, convents. She was assisted in her labours by kindred spirits, such as Juan of the Cross, the reformer of the male Carmelites, and

*St. Teresa.*

Jerome Gratian of the Mother of God, whose appointment to the visitorship of all the Carmelites of Andalusia gave rise to the conflict between the reformed and the unreformed sections of the order which so greatly troubled St. Teresa's later years. She would not have been victorious in the end, when Gregory XIII. severed the discalced from the mitigated Carmelites (1580), had it not been for the support of King Philip. From the charges brought against her a few years earlier, by personal spite or folly, and taken up by the Inquisition, she had easily cleared herself.

The efforts of St. Teresa during the last fifteen years of her life, and their hard-won success, would go far to account for the influence exercised by her upon her contemporaries. But she had also found time to compose those prose manuals of devotion—more especially the *Interior Castle*, a kind of Catholic castle of *Mansoul*—which might almost be described as the popular text-books of Spanish mysticism. Far removed alike from quietism and from pantheism, she is practical in the midst of her elevated piety, and a 'mild and milky' humankindness percolates the intensity of her enthusiasm. Thus the ecstatic visionary who beheld the Saviour at her right hand may be numbered among those who, with clear eye and humble heart, have toiled to advance His cause among men, because the divine love of which she thought herself a chosen witness was the love that bears fruit in action.

The spirit of unworldly and unselfish piety which animated much of the religious life of Spain in this period was likewise actively at work in the very centre of the hierarchical system of the Church of Rome. The reforms of the Council of Trent proved far from ineffective, and Rome herself, amidst all the dangers and disturbances through which that city passed, assumed and maintained an aspect befitting her religious pretensions. The Tridentine decrees, with their prohibitions of non-residence, pluralities, and other profitable abuses, could not, in the nature of the case, be generally popular at Rome. But they found loyal upholders in the Popes, encouraged as they were in their attitude by the Spanish king, upon whom the three predecessors of Sixtus V. consistently leant. The simplicity—under Pius V. it might be called austerity —of the Papal court in this period contrasts with the easy luxury of earlier and the formal grandeur of later days. If the Papal government under Gregory XIII. pressed its feudal rights home with undue vigour, the Christian world at large was no longer aggrieved by a system of scandalous exactions. The College of Cardinals underwent a similar change, and not only in externals, as to which Cardinal Borromeo had set a salutary example. The restrictions imposed by the conciliar decrees combined with the large increase in the number of the members of the Sacred College to diminish simultaneously the importance and the attractions of the dignity; and even under Clement VIII. (1592–1605), according to Bellarmine, the households of most of the cardinals were established on no extravagant footing.

*The Counter-Reformation at Rome.*

As a matter of course, the strength of the current varied according to the circumstances of the successive pontificates, and more especially according to the character of each successive Pope. Pius V. (1566-72) carried into St. Peter's chair the traditions of the order of St. Dominic. As Cardinal Ghislieri, he had held the office of Inquisitor-general at Rome during the two previous pontificates, and no break in the activity of the Inquisition ensued on his elevation. Under him the Tridentine decrees became a working test, from which he allowed no prelate, priest, or monastic order to remain exempt; while the Inquisition was encouraged to call to account even the highest dignitaries of the most loyal churches, such as the Archbishop of Toledo. The Pope's religious zeal knew no bounds as to the duties which he imposed upon either himself or others; and such were the purity and holiness of the conduct of his life, both public and private, that his canonisation in later days (1712) admits of no cavil. He was the sworn foe of nepotism, and his bull *Admonet nos* (1567) prohibited for ever the alienation of any fief of the Church, thus setting the example of the *non possumus* since steadily maintained. In his foreign policy, too, he was essentially consistent. In 1568 he reissued with additions the bull *In cœnâ Domini*, which explicitly asserted the claims of the Papacy to the supreme control of the states of the world. He congratulated Alva on the efficiency of his Council of Blood, and exhorted Charles IX. to pull up the Huguenot heresy by the very fibres of its roots (1569). He took part in the French wars with money and men; and while he spared no pains to animate the lukewarm loyalty of the Emperor Maximilian II. towards the Church, he was ready to cut off from it a rebellious member like Queen Elizabeth

(1570), and to interest himself in the plots directed against her life. The supreme effort of his European policy was the formation of the league between Spain and Venice, which resulted in the naval victory of Lepanto (1571), memorable to Catholic Christianity for all succeeding times, nor, to do Pius V. justice, barren of practical results by his fault.

Gregory XIII. (Buoncompagni), who followed Pius V. in the Papal chair, was chiefly occupied with the fearful excesses of the banditti, and with the pretensions of their good friends and patrons, the baronage of the Roman States. Though unsuccessful in his attempt to put an end to the anarchy around him, he gravitated back in some measure towards that propitiatory system from which it was difficult for the temporal power to shake itself free, even when, as in his case, it no longer had dynastic aims in view. Yet, as he prudently refrained from seeking to maintain the full rigour of the discipline introduced by his predecessor into the life of Church and laity, Rome, which under him largely increased in the numbers of its inhabitants, no longer felt doomed to decline, but could more easily reconcile itself with the reformatory movement. By the spirit of that movement Gregory's ecclesiastical policy was essentially animated. Not only did he encourage life-long labours like those of Philip of Neri (1515–95), which clothed in a garb of humorous cheerfulness the heroism of self-sacrifice, but he neither concealed his belief, nor spared expenditure to prove it, that the Papacy ought to be a combative power. He hailed with open satisfaction the news of the Massacre of St. Bartholomew (1572), and sent forth

*Gregory XIII.*

the mission to England (1580), of which no historian has as yet fully demonstrated the significance. He was active both in advancing the propagation of the faith in distant lands and in the endowment of churches and the establishment of colleges nearer home. His interest in the promotion of clerical education was more especially noteworthy; and, herein thoroughly in accordance with the Jesuits, whom he specially favoured, he helped to carry into effect one of the most important of the principles approved by the Council of Trent. Even the promulgation of the Calendar which bears his name (1582) would suffice to disprove his having been the *papa negativus*, the Pope of mere intentions, as which he was derided by Roman wit.

It was, however, with Sixtus V. (Montalto) that, as the very legends clustering round the history of his origin and election seem to testify, the full vigour and self-reliance of the Papal government once more renewed themselves. Already in the earliest years of his manhood, when known throughout Italy as an eloquent and fearless popular preacher, he became one of the most active labourers in the cause of the Catholic Reformation, and excited the interest of the future Popes Paul IV. and Pius V., as well as of Loyola and of Philip of Neri. The severity with which he afterwards reformed the convents of his brother Franciscans at Siena, Naples, and Venice further raised his reputation at Rome; but at Venice, where he for a time acted as Inquisitor, the Seigniory in the end demanded and obtained his recall. He was afterwards appointed vicar-general of his order at Rome,

*Sixtus V.*

and lost no opportunity of continuing his strife against
the backward and the lukewarm. His journey to Spain
as theologian to Cardinal Buoncompagni (afterwards
Pope Gregory XIII.), on his mission for the settlement
of Carranza's case, led to disputes which long left their
sting. When Montalto, whom Pius V. had raised to
the cardinalate, came forth from the retirement into
which he had withdrawn under Gregory's pontificate,
the change in him was assuredly due to no previous
dissimulation. Indeed, of hypocrisy there was no trace
in his brusque and coarse nature; for such it certainly remained, notwithstanding his delight in books
and the arts, especially architecture, which under him
added so largely to the grandeur as well as to the
orthodoxy of the aspect of Rome. His earliest success was the complete restoration of order in the Papal
states as against the banditti and their protectors.
His financial arrangements in conjunction with the
frugality of his expenditure secured to his government
a large annual surplus. His bull *Immensa æterna Dei*
reorganised the whole pontifical system of government by a careful distribution of its functions among
fifteen Congregations or committees of cardinals, of
which the first was the Holy Office, charged with the
control of all matters of faith, and presided over by the
Pope in person. Another bull (*Postquam verus ille*)
fixed the number of cardinals at seventy. Though
on the whole his creations were confined to men of
eminent piety and reforming opinions, he was unable
to escape altogether the ἀνάγκη of the temporal power,
and his nephew, the youthful Cardinal Montalto, came
to be his chief minister for foreign affairs, and indeed

for matters of state in general. For the rest, no sovereign was ever more his own master. He endeavoured to maintain an active communication with the bishops without constantly interfering with their diocesan authority, and he was not afraid of modifying on occasion even the privileges of the Inquisition. As for the Jesuits, he treated them coolly, and placed on the Index a work of their redoubtable controversialist Bellarmine.

Sixtus V. frequently declared his desire for a great crusade against the Turk, but he can hardly be supposed to have intended the treasures hoarded by him to be exhausted by this object. His first overtures were inevitably made to Philip II., whom, however, he found to be intent upon very different aims. He could not gainsay the logical necessity of a Spanish invasion of England, though he would have preferred, had it been possible, the conversion of Queen Elizabeth, between whom and himself there prevailed an odd kind of mutual regard. He promised a large annual subsidy to Philip; but the failure of the Armada materially diminished his respect for the King, whom, together with his ambassador Olivarez, he heartily disliked, and who had offended him by his claim to regulate ecclesiastical titles in Spain. At the same time Sixtus V. never thought either of making war upon Philip or of attempting, like Paul IV., to wrest Naples from his hands. His foes were the foes of the Church, such as Geneva, which he at first encouraged Charles Emmanuel of Savoy to attack, and his friends were her friends, such as King Stephen Bathory of Poland (1575–86), on whose death, followed by the accession of the

Swedish Sigismund, he warmly interested himself in the maintenance of Catholicism in Poland at its re-establishment in Sweden. But nowhere had the political energy of Sixtus V. so difficult a field of action as in France, which he was anxious both to preserve to the Church and to prevent from becoming a dependency of Spain.

Whether or not it be true that the first of the religious wars of France (1562-63) preserved France from becoming a Huguenot country, at all events after the Convention of Amboise (March 1563) such a result was no longer possible. Pius IV.'s angry schemes of *revanche* were dropped at the instance of the French crown; nor is there any evidence to show that at the Conference of Bayonne (June 1565) a plan was concocted for the complete recovery of France for Catholicism with the aid of Spain and Rome. But the extirpation of Protestantism throughout the monarchy was certainly counselled there, and before long auxiliaries were sent by Alva from the Netherlands, and a large subsidy was promised by Philip if Charles IX. would continue the war (January 1568). Thus the struggle against the Huguenots soon assumed a complexion in harmony with the conceptions of Philip of Spain and with the Counter-Reformation movement. A league for the extirpation of heresy was established at Toulouse under the name of a crusade (September 1568), and the fanaticism of the Catholic preachers was revived on no less primitive a type. The victory of Jarnac and the death of Condé (13th March 1569) elicited from the delighted Pius V. admonitions to Charles IX.

*The religious struggle in France.*

to tear up not only the roots of the evil, but the very fibres of the roots. But the cool selfishness of Catharine de' Medici and her sons contributed almost as much as the heroic pertinacity of the Huguenots to avert such a doom from France. The Peace of St. Germain (1570) was sincerely meant by Charles IX., the policy of whose government was at this time so far removed from subservience to Spain as to be in direct contact with Elizabeth of England, with William of Orange, and with Coligny himself. The friends of the Catholic reaction felt that so dangerous a tendency must be arrested; and the proposed marriage between the sister of the king and the young Huguenot King of Navarre was as odious to Pope Pius V. as it was to the bigoted populace of Paris. Yet the immediate responsibility of the Massacre of St. Bartholomew (24th August 1572) cannot be shifted from the shoulders where it rests. The origin of the crime has to be sought, not in the fanaticism of the Guises, but in Catharine de' Medici's jealousy of Coligny's influence over the King, and in the momentary impulse which stirred up Charles to act for himself. The fire once lit, found inflammatory matter in abundance in the bigoted capital and in other parts of the country. The news of the massacre, received with joy and thanksgiving by Philip II. and the new Pope, Gregory XIII., could not fail to intensify with unprecedented force the bitterness of the religious conflict in France, and in Europe generally. But the religious policy of the French Government continued wavering, and during the remainder of the reign of Charles IX. by no means identified itself with the aims of the reaction. On the accession of

Henry III. (1574), there was much uncertainty as to what influence would establish itself over his shallow and unstable mind, whether that of the tolerant Maximilian II. and the Doge Mocenigo, or that of Pope Gregory and the Cardinal of Lorraine, now near his end (December 1574). At first he seemed prepared to use force against the Huguenots, and Jesuit and other influences induced him to set on foot a kind of Counter-Reformation on his own account, during which the Flagellants were violently brought into fashion. But this, of course, could not last; and in the so-called Peace of Monsieur (1576) terms were granted to the Huguenots that caused a loud outcry at Paris and elsewhere, to which the Guises were no strangers. Thus arose the Holy League (1576), which had been preceded by analogous associations, but soon, with the aid both of the Jesuits and in more popular spheres of the Franciscans, absorbed in itself all the minor confederacies. Whether or not the League from the first pursued the design of supplanting the King by Henry, Duke of Guise, its origin was certainly native, though the name of Philip of Spain was before long associated with its operations.

The changes in the attitude of the wretched Henry III. towards the League and towards the Huguenots which ensued show him writhing under an unbearable incubus. The death of his even more contemptible brother Anjou (1581), shortly after, in the Peace of Fleix, favourable terms had been granted to the Huguenots, gave to the Protestant Henry of Navarre the next hereditary claim to the throne, and at the same time seemed to call upon the League and its supporters to accomplish both their avowed and their secret objects. Thus the understanding—agreement—plot—was matured, to which the chiefs of the League, the Guises in particular, and Philip of Spain were parties. In 1584, they, together with Charles Emmanuel of Savoy, entered into a compact amounting to a scheme for subduing France, in part by foreign arms. Only a year earlier, Pope Gregory's demand for the introduction into France of the whole of the Tridentine decrees had been accompanied by a large influx of Jesuits, and an organisation of the League had been established at Paris, which, in complete understanding with the Guises, evoked the spirit of the commune to aid in the destruction of the national monarchy. Henry III. now entreated Henry of Navarre to abjure the profession of the Protestant faith which barred his succession to the throne; for in the Treaty of Joinville (January 1585), Spain, the Guises, and the Cardinal of Bourbon united in support of the Cardinal's candidature for the now vacant throne, and of the exclusion of all heretic princes, while the aid of Spain was promised to the League.

Sixtus V., surrounded by Hispaniolising cardinals, at first continued to aim at a reconciliation between the Catholic League and Henry III., and was even induced to publish a depriving bull against Navarre and Condé (September 1585). But he had been gradually cooling towards the League, which so openly menaced the independence of the French monarchy, when the assassination by the King's orders of the Guises changed the aspect of affairs (September 1588). The Pope could not avoid calling the unhappy King to account at

*Sixtus V., Henry IV., and Spain.*

least for the murder of the Cardinal; but the assassination of Henry III. himself (August 1589) once more introduced a change in the situation. For a time it seemed necessary to go hand in hand with Spain in opposing the accession of Henry of Navarre. 'The Catholic faith,' said Sixtus, 'is even nearer to our heart than France.' But Henry had resolved upon his course, and the assurances of his agent, Luxemburg, found a ready listener in the Pope. During the lifetime of the Cardinal of Bourbon, whom the Leaguers recognised as King Charles X., the policy of Sixtus was accordingly one of postponement. On the Cardinal's death (May 1590), no escape remained from one of two alternatives —Henry IV., or some vassal pure and simple of Spain. It was then that Philip II. proposed to the Pope a definitive treaty of alliance, of which the latter delayed the signature till his hand was cold in death. Before Sixtus V. passed away (27th August 1590) it had become clear that he would be no party to the Spanish bargain. So far as in her lay, Rome had saved France from Spain.

During the thirty years covered by these pontificates the movement of the Counter-Reformation in Italy had thus in the main followed the lines and employed the agencies adopted by it in the previous period. The results produced were of that mixed character with which partisan history has no patience, combining as they did the edifying influence of lives and labours like those of St. Charles Borromeo and St. Philip of Neri with the morally and intellectually deadening effect of Inquisition and Index. Doubtless examples of saintly lives are to be found in many periods of Italian history

*Moral and intellectual effects of the Counter-Reformation in Italy.*

besides this; but, on the other hand, neither was the decay of learning and letters in Italy entirely owing to the Holy Office, or even to the complete establishment in this period of the control of Spain over a large part of the peninsula. The Renascence had to a great extent worked itself out; nor is there sufficient reason for the assumption that the Italian mind in general was prepared to turn with compensatory zeal to those scientific studies which the reaction held in especial abhorrence. The steady progress and extension of the operations of the Jesuits, more especially in the sphere of higher education, which reached its height under Gregory XIII., indisputably contributed to diminish the mental vigour of the nation. For the freedom of the Renascence, or the license into which it had too easily degenerated, was substituted a system even less defensible than the hard exclusiveness of the Inquisition—a method of reduction, expurgation, emasculation, which shrank from nothing because it could assimilate everything. Italian literature shows unmistakable signs of this influence, though it may savour of exaggeration to attribute the blending of sensuousness with pietism in Torquato Tasso (1544–95) to the principles instilled into him as a boy by the Jesuits. Nor has it proved difficult to show that Italian art, plastic, pictorial, and musical, begins in this period to exhibit the same impress. Even more wide-reaching is the question, whether the continuance (for it was in any case a continuance) of the moral corruption of Italian society is to be ascribed, as it has been from Fra Paolo downwards, to Jesuit misdirection of consciences. Statistics (even when perfectly trustworthy) of crime and immorality, of brigandage and piracy, of social disorganisation and superstitious remedies hardly less pernicious than the disease, must be viewed as results of many contributory causes. The yoke of the foreigner and the ascendancy of his influence over all national aspirations, the weakness of native, and, especially before Sixtus V., of ecclesiastical government, the contempt, of which the later Italian Renascence had set the fashion, for mere moral restraints, and the ineradicable tendency of human things to go from bad to worse—all these causes should be taken into account together with the deteriorating influences attributed with good reason to much of the Jesuit teaching of this age. No authoritative exposition of its principles sanctioning any more advanced developement of them was, however, in this period put forth by the Society, which had good reason to be on its guard under Popes so unfavourable to it as Pius V. and Sixtus V.

In the great struggle carried on by the Counter-Reformation from these centres the resistance opposed to it varied alike in character and in results.

*The Counter-Reformation and the revolt of the Netherlands.* In France the end was a compromise of which time alone could test the value; in the Netherlands, an enduring schism; in England and the Scandinavian North, national defiance. There remained the debateable land of Central Europe. The progress of the conflict in France has been already touched upon. From first to last, the struggle here was much affected by the course of the revolt of the Netherlands, which largely owed its origin to religious causes. It has been asserted that the real cause of the insurrection was the selfish discontent of the nobility.

Moreover, it has been argued that Philip merely carried out the edicts periodically promulgated by his father; nor, in truth, had the Reformation at the time of his accession obtained much real hold over the inhabitants of the Provinces at large. The slowness of the earlier advance of Protestantism in this quarter is, however, sufficiently explained by the character of the population, while the religious Peace of Augsburg helps to account for the comparative rapidity of its extension about the time in question. Again, how could the increased activity of religious persecution early in Philip's reign, when the government of the Provinces was becoming wholly Spanish, fail to excite the most serious fears that, notwithstanding the King's denial (1562), the establishment of the *Spanish* Inquisition was actually intended? For a moment it seemed, under the government of Margaret of Parma, that a measure of concessions might be obtained by Egmont at Madrid (1565). But Philip protested before the crucifix that he would never call himself master of recreants, and sent instructions for the continuance of the persecution, and for the enforcement (with the usual reservations) of the Tridentine decrees. An emigration of some 30,000 persons ensued, and the troubles began (1566). By midsummer all seemed over, and the May edict, demanding summary immediate death against the preachers of the reformed religion, triumphant. Yet it was Alva's arrival (August 1567), and the excesses of authority ensuing, which led to the outbreak of the real struggle (1568). The 'Council of Blood,' to whose extreme penalty, by the sentence of the Inquisition and subsequent royal proclamation, all the inhabitants of the Netherlands were, as declared heretics, rendered obnoxious (Feb. 1568), is reckoned to have during the seven years of Alva's government doomed 18,000 human beings to death by the executioner's hands. In Alva, even had not the Papal blessing expressly descended upon the symbols of his military authority, popular feeling recognised the agent of Rome not less than the servant of Spain, and through him the revolt of the Netherlands was definitively stamped as both a popular and a religious uprising. The peace negotiations at Breda (1575) came to a speedy end on the religious question, and it was as exclusively Protestant communities that these Provinces formally emancipated themselves from Spanish control under the stadtholderate of William of Orange (1575-76). It was again the religious question that largely helped to break up the wider confederation,. which, in the Pacification of Ghent (1576), included, together with these northern, fifteen southern provinces. After the emigration in Alva's days, the large majority of the inhabitants in the southern provinces were Catholics. They were found ready to abolish the Inquisition and to annul the obnoxious edicts of Charles V.; but they conceded no more than the liberty of private worship to the Protestants, and thereby shut the door upon the emigrants. Under the administration of Don John of Austria (1576-78), whose mind was wholly set upon a great naval expedition for the liberation of Mary Queen of Scots, Orange attempted to maintain the national union against Spain on the basis of mutual tolerance between Protestants and Catholics (December 1577; but his noble and unique endeavour must have failed even had it not been for Alexander Farnese's victory of Gemblours (January 1578). Under Parma's own administration (1578–92) the separation of North and South was accomplished. The Union of Utrecht (1579), though it left the door open to the Catholic provinces, announced the inevitable dualism, and in the same year the sack of Maestricht decided the Walloons to return to their allegiance to Philip of Spain, and to exclude all forms of faith but the Roman Catholic. The Peace Congress at Cologne dissolved itself (1580), and the United Provinces renounced the sovereignty of the 'tyrant' who claimed to be their ruler. The events which followed made no change in these general relations. In 1584 the victories of Parma led to the submission of Flanders and to the restoration of Catholicism there, with a reservation to the Protestants of the right of private worship. The death of Anjou, whose contemptible part had been played out, and the murder of William of Orange, were indeed followed by further negotiations with France, but they were cut short by the capitulation of Brussels to Parma (March 1585); and the fate of the whole of the Southern Netherlands was decided by the fall of Antwerp (August). The city was speedily re-Catholicised with the help of the Jesuits, and with it the Belgic provinces were permanently lost to the Union and to Protestantism.

*The dualism established.*

During nine further years the struggle continued before, by the restoration of the whole of the United Provinces to independence, the balance between them and the Spanish Netherlands was finally adjusted. In the earlier of these years Parma's powers were crippled by the armaments for the invasion of England, in which he was to have taken part. During the remainder of his life the intervention of Spain in the French civil war obliged him to postpone the reconquest of the Netherlands, as well as the conquest of England; and his death (December 1592) closed the prospect of any further advance of the Counter-Reformation in the Low Countries. From 1594 the war against Spain becomes an international war. If in the very province (Holland) which had been the mainstay of the great revolt may be descried, half a century later, the traces of a Catholic reaction powerful enough to command the adherence of the favourite national poet (Joost van den Vondel), this movement must be viewed as an inevitable intellectual revolt against the rigid Calvinism which triumphed over the Arminians at Dort (1618–19).

Both Rome and the Escurial convinced themselves very slowly of the delusiveness of the hope that Queen Elizabeth would adhere to the Church re-established in England by her sister; nor could Sixtus V. bring himself to despair of her conversion. Whatever may have been the secret wishes of the majority of the English clergy, the pendulum of public opinion after her accession swung strongly in the Protestant direction. Even in Lancashire it needed the personal exertions of William (afterwards Cardinal) Allen to arrest the practice of conformity in his native county (1562). From this time forward the English mission periodically attracted the efforts of Catholic zeal, and English Jesuits were sporadically engaged in missionary labours in this country. But the first enduring impulse in this direction was

*The Catholic Propaganda in England.*

given by the establishment, through the zeal of Allen and others, of an English College in the University of Douay in 1568. This was the year in which Mary Queen of Scots became a fugitive and a prisoner in England, after in Scotland the Parliament which had accepted her forced resignation had done its utmost to accomplish the extirpation of the Roman faith. Before the year was out, the first plots for her liberation had been formed, and the struggle for the English throne had begun. Her release formed part of the programme of the rebellion of the Northern Earls, who took up arms for the restoration of the Catholic religion under the banner of the Five Wounds of Christ (1569); it was she who was to take the place of Elizabeth, excommunicated by the bull of Pius V. (1570), and doomed to a violent death by the Ridolfi plot (1571). The manager of this latter scheme was armed with credentials from the Pope to commend him to the Catholic nobility of England. The foundation of the English College at Douay, significant as the earliest result of the Tridentine decree on clerical seminaries, was of special moment for the course of the religious struggle in England. Driven away for some years from Douay (1578–93), the college was speedily re-established at Rheims under the protection of the Guises and with a subvention from Philip II. To Allen, who superintended the management of the college in both places, was likewise due the reorganisation of the English College at Rome (1579), originally an offshoot of Douay. And it was under his influence that Gregory XIII. allowed the Jesuit mission to go forth, which in April 1580 left

*The English Colleges.*

Rome for England under the leadership of Robert Parsons and of Edmund Campion, afterwards (December 1581) its protomartyr. Most of its members had been trained at Douay; many, before they had resided here, or at Rheims, Paris and Rome, had been members of an English university, more generally of Oxford. Large numbers followed in their wake; according to an authorised computation, 250 Catholic priests were sent into England within the years 1575 to 1585 only; and sixty of these suffered martyrdom. Those who suffered death in these years were executed for denying the Queen's ecclesiastical supremacy; they were therefore punished as traitors, though many of them, when interrogated on the subject at their trials, steadily professed their recognition of the Queen as their lawful sovereign. The rigour of these persecutions was increased by the discovery of the plots against the Queen's life, which in 1584 led to the formation of the association, sanctioned by Act of Parliament, for the protection of her life, and, if need were, for revenge upon those who had taken it. Many suffered under another Act ordering Jesuits and other seminary priests to leave the kingdom within forty days, under the penalty of treason. With the Jesuits the memories of Catholic martyrdom in England pre-eminently connect themselves; the special rigour shown towards the members of the order surrounded it with so glorious a halo in the eyes of the zealous, that many caused themselves to be received into it when actually face to face with death.

*The Jesuit mission of 1580.*

And as the English propaganda of the Jesuits continued, their colleges in Flanders, Lorraine, Spain, and elsewhere increased and multiplied, till a whole series of refuges stood open to the expatriated. Yet the Jesuits had no monopoly of martyrdom; many other priests suffered death and the tortures which preceded or accompanied it, while the recusancy statutes of this and the following reign placed a considerable proportion of the gentry of the land within the walls of its prisons. To what extent the steady endurance shown by so many Catholic families in England was due to the Elizabethan propaganda, and to what extent the Catholic revival of the days of James I. and Charles I. was prepared by it, cannot be easily determined. In any case, the fruits of the Counter-Reformation in England were not all gathered in when the great issues of the European conflict seemed to decide themselves—when Duessa was caught in the toils, and the great Armada came and was dissipated.

Among the designs elaborated at Rome, in the Jesuit colleges and in the family council of the Guises, had been the intrigue of which Esmé Stuart, Count d'Aubigny, whom James VI. created Earl of Lennox, was the central figure. Its object was to restore French influence, and thus gradually to re-establish a Catholic ascendancy in Scotland, to be followed by the association of the liberated Mary with her son in its government, and perhaps by a marriage between Lennox and Arabella Stuart, always a possible claimant for the English throne. The plan was, however, misliked by Philip II., and extinguished by the Raid of Ruthven (1582), which had at its back a solid popular resistance.

*A Catholic reaction in Scotland.*

Very different, of course, was the state of religious feeling in Ireland, where a long series of popular insurrections (Ulster 1565, Munster 1569, Connaught 1577) had exposed the hollowness of Elizabeth's Protestant Establishment. But though the eyes of the Irish had long turned to Spain, Philip hesitated about taking any measures tending to sever the connexion between England and Ireland; nor was it till 1579 that the outrages of Drake effectively supplemented the arguments urged upon the King two years before by Nicholas Sanders. After Sanders and his companions had landed in Kerry and the insurrection of Desmond had broken out, Philip connived at the despatch of a slight reinforcement from Spain (1580), but only with the result of causing the massacre of Smerwick. In Tyrone's insurrection Spain co-operated late and ineffectively (1602). Thus the Counter-Reformation cannot be said to have availed itself to much purpose of the vantage-ground offered to it by the loyalty of the Irish people to the Church of Rome.

*Spanish attempts in Ireland.*

In one of the Scandinavian kingdoms an attempt was made within this period to bring about a reaction towards Rome, but under conditions almost prohibitory of permanent success. Gustavus Vasa (1523-60), the liberator of Sweden, had at Westerås in 1529 completely transferred to himself the supreme authority in matters ecclesiastical. The episcopal system came to a virtual, and the monasteries to an absolute, end. The nobility was largely gained for the Reformation by being allowed a share in the spoils, and the people's assent was won

*Attempt at a Counter-Reformation by John III. of Sweden.*

over rather than forced; for in the reign of Gustavus I., which counts so many political victims, the penalty of death was never undergone for the sake of religion. But under John III. (1569–92) a reaction was attempted. John had overthrown his elder brother, the unhappy Eric XIV., in alliance with his younger brother, Charles, whose authority, though he had formally renounced his claim to a share of the throne, more or less overshadowed it till he actually seated himself there. While Charles steadily professed his adherence to the national Church as founded by their father upon the Bible, the attitude of John towards the religious question contributed materially to endanger his tenure of the throne. Possessed of some theological learning, John at first showed a desire to unite the contending religions on the basis of the tenets and usages of the primitive Church, and of concessions such as those contained in the Augsburg Interim, which had been already rejected by Sweden in 1549; but the result was, that while the nation remained unmoved, the King himself, largely influenced by his beloved consort, Catharine, a daughter of Sigismund I. of Poland, drifted nearer and nearer to Rome. As early as 1572 Cardinal Hosius was full of his praises, and in 1576 he commissioned two Jesuits, under the guise of Lutheran preachers, to work upon Swedish opinion. Hereupon the Counter-Reformation began, favoured by King John, but in so uncertain a fashion as to disquiet Pope Gregory XIII., who disapproved of the tortuous proceedings of the Jesuits, and called upon the King openly to profess the Catholic faith. He preferred, however, to promulgate his

Liturgy or Red Book (1576), which was based upon the missal approved at Trent and edited by the Jesuits, with a view to preparing the complete resumption of the mass. At the diet of 1577, the most violent of the recalcitrants having been removed, both clergy and lay estates, with few exceptions, gave in the required adhesion. But the King's special envoy, Pontus de la Gardie, failed to obtain Gregory XIII.'s assent to the policy of gradual conversion, accompanied by interimistic concessions (the marriage of priests and the Communion in both kinds for the laity), and by conformity on the part of the King to heretical worship; and the Jesuit Possevin was sent to Sweden to urge a more decided course. Whether or not he actually received John into the Church of Rome (at Wadstena in 1578), the Counter-Reformation now progressed with much greater openness. Luther's Catechism was banished from the schools; the Bishop of Linköping was publicly divested of the insignia of his office for calling the Pope Antichrist; the archiepiscopate was kept vacant for four years, and while Jesuits continued to preach with so much audacity as to incur reprimands from the Council of State, a number of Swedish youths were sent abroad to be trained in the faith of Rome. But before long the King's zeal began to cool. He had been disappointed in the political expectations he had founded on the influence of Rome (especially in the matter of the peace between Russia and Poland, concluded under the mediation of Possevin in 1582), and the death of Queen Catharine (1583) completed the estrangement. Soon the Jesuits were expelled the realm, and all converts to Rome were threatened with banishment. When John's heir, Sigismund, was elected King of Poland (1587), his father exhorted him not to bind himself in obedience to the Pope. John himself, after indulging in the fleeting project of union with the Greek Church, clung to the compromise of his 'Red Book.' But now this liturgy met with widespread resistance; clergymen who shrank from it were deposed, imprisoned, or banished, and more turbulent opponents paid the penalty of their lives. While the King embittered the conflict by personal violence, his brother, Duke Charles, openly stood forth as the adversary of his innovations. In 1592 King John died, sick at heart of the results of his futile endeavour to reconcile extremes by his royal *fiat*. On his death Lutheranism was reintroduced, and a kind of covenant for its maintenance adopted by a mixed clerical and lay assembly at Upsala (1593); nor were its results permanently affected by the coronation visit (1593-94) of the Catholic King Sigismund, accompanied by the Papal legate Malaspina. The struggle between Sigismund and his uncle Charles which followed forms part of the European religious conflict. Charles IX., as from 1604 he formally consented to be called, had before this maintained a diplomatic intercourse with Elizabeth and Henry IV., and in 1608 sought an alliance with the United Provinces. His attempt to establish Swedish Protestantism on a broader basis than that of the Augsburg Confession was defeated by the decree of the Upsala Assembly of 1607.

No attempt at a Catholic reaction followed upon the establishment of the Reformation in Denmark by Christian III. (1536); and both in his reign and in that of his successor, Frederick II. (1559-88), Danish Protestantism grew typically intolerant. In 1554, the year after John a Lasco and a large number of other fugitives from the Marian persecutions had been refused shelter at Copenhagen, Christian III. prescribed that all strangers should satisfy the authorities on the subject of their faith before being allowed to settle in Denmark; and in 1559 Frederick II. promulgated a confession of faith which was to serve as a uniform test on such occasions. It had been drawn up at the suggestion of Jacob Andreæ, a rigid Lutheran theologian, recommended to Frederick by his brother-in-law, the Elector Augustus of Saxony. Yet the celebrated *Formula concordiæ*, by which the latter sought to extinguish all Protestant disunion, King Frederick threw into the fire.

*Protestant intolerance in Denmark.*

Beyond a doubt the variations of Protestantism which both these princes desired to reduce or to remove are to be reckoned among the causes which contributed to the progress of the Counter-Reformation. The Catholic reaction of the sixteenth century benefited by the disunion produced among the Protestants through variety of dogma, just as it profited by the scandals of the Reformation (the divorce of Henry VIII., the bigamy of Philip of Hesse), and by the greed of Church lands patent in many of the princes who adopted it. With regard, however, to the variations of Protestantism, their illustrious historian, Bossuet, assuredly vindicates their right of existence when he traces them to their real source. Luther, by insisting on the doctrine of

*The divisions among Protestants as aids of the Counter-Reformation.*

the universal priesthood of Christian believers, laid the axe at the root of the mighty growth which had for centuries overshadowed the religious life of the nations. Henceforth, accordingly, theologians of every Protestant sect emulously strove to find a generally acceptable definition of the visible Church. Neither, however, could the Catholic definition, according to which the Church has always professed the same truth through all its members, any longer be upheld without a great variety of explanations and interpretations, by no means always obviously consistent with one another. Still, even before the Council of Trent had promulgated its dogmatic decrees, it was on the Protestant side that the variations of doctrine had been most striking, most frequent, and most perplexing to pious souls. The very Augsburg Confession (1530), while in a sense conceived in a spirit of conciliation towards Rome, marked with perfect distinctness the divergence between the doctrinal position of the Lutherans and that of the Zwinglians, and led, as if designedly, to the *Confessio tetrapolitana*, which in its turn defined the Zwinglian standpoint with unprecedented plainness (1531). Bucer's surrender on the cardinal subject of the Eucharist in the Wittenberg *Concordia* (1536) was not ratified by more than a section of the Zwinglian Churches. Calvin, who about this time began the work of his life, exerted himself at Ratisbon (1541) to keep Melanchthon firm against concession to Rome; but the schism remained unhealed, and two years before his death Luther did his utmost to render it permanent by reasserting in their harshest form his views

*Lutheranism and Calvinism in the Empire.*

on the Eucharistic question (1544). Luther's death itself encouraged the tendency to disunion with which the application to religious matters of the principle of territorial sovereignty so completely fell in. Even among the Protestant princes and cities of the Augsburg Confession each claimed the right of determining the precise nature of their subjects' creed, after causing it to be defined by the court or city preacher, or by the divinity faculty in the local university. In short the principle, '*Cujus est regio, ejus est religio,*' was asserted with perfect frankness. As between the Lutherans and Calvinists, the fact that the religious peace of Augsburg included the former alone created an unprecedented bitterness, while their political interests began to diverge as widely as their confessional tenets. Hence a desire on both sides to find the clearest formal expression for existing dogmatic differences—an eagerness quite in harmony with the spirit of the contemporary Inquisition in Spain and Italy to purge each territorial or local Church from elements regarded as strange or intrusive, and a persecution at last too frequently carried on for its own sake. In the Empire, the religious division among the Protestants soon acquired a very marked political significance, more especially after Frederick III., Elector Palatine, had, by the promulgation of the *Heidelberg Catechism* in 1562, taken his natural place at the head of the Calvinists, and had sent a large force under his son, John Casimir, to aid the French Huguenots (1567), thus opening the long political drama which ended with the catastrophe of his great-grandson, Frederick V. The Calvinist era in the Palatinate is marked by ruthless intolerance, and the execution of Silvanus at Heidelberg (1573) is hardly less typical than is the burning of Servetus at Geneva twenty years before. The headquarters of the most rigid Lutheran orthodoxy were for a time at Jena, where Flacius, to whom the systematisation of Lutheranism is largely due, resided till 1561, in the service of the ill-used Ernestine line of the Saxon house. He found an unrelenting enemy in the head of the Albertine line, the Elector Augustus, who in the earlier part of his reign (1553–86) attempted to maintain a moderate Lutheran attitude; but his opinions afterwards stiffened: he became the promulgator of the *Formula concordiæ* of 1580, and harried his own 'crypto-Calvinists' with so deadly a zeal, that hopes were indulged at Rome of his ultimate conversion to the Catholic Church. In the case of the Brandenburg Albert, who, before converting East Prussia into a secular duchy, had introduced the Reformation there, the Lutheran bigotry displayed by his clergy and nobility against Osiander and the Osiandrists, culminating in the execution of his own confessor (Funcke) in the midst of a psalm-singing mob, lent more colour to the report that he had died a Roman Catholic (1568). These currents of feeling perverted even the very attempts made to combine them into a common stream. Of the numerous formulæ of belief composed, in more or less sincerity, with such a design during the latter half of the sixteenth century, the earliest was Melanchthon's (1559), who died in the following year, without having accomplished his long and much-misunderstood endeavour to reunite Christendom. Soon the hope passed away of a recon-

*margin: The Formula Concordiæ.*

ciliation, such as might have warranted the schemes of a general Protestant League, which prompted Queen Elizabeth's message to Heidelberg (1577) and Ségur's German mission when the French religious struggle was at its height (1584). For the object of the notorious *Formula concordiæ* of 1580—notorious because of the means employed to enforce it—was speedily perceived to be the repression of all Philippist and trimming as well as of Calvinist doctrine. It was signed by the majority of the Protestant Estates of the Empire and by several thousands of theologians; but the Calvinists, who refused it, had the moral support of Elizabeth of England, of Henry of Navarre, and of Augustus of Saxony's own brother-in-law, Frederick II. of Denmark; while a significant comment upon it was furnished by the breach opened about this time (1585-87) in the Netherlands between the Calvinists and the less rigidly disposed adherents of the Reformation.

*Protestant heterodoxy.* Meanwhile a school or tendency of Protestant thought and opinion began to become perceptible, of which the seeds had been blown hither and thither —northwards at first and westwards—by the blast of persecution, and on which the anathemas of the Churches both old and new called down the repressive force of the secular arm. During the earlier times of the Reformation these often isolated efforts had been officially and popularly lumped together as Anabaptism; in this later period more than one noteworthy endeavour of the kind came from those Latin countries where the activity of the Counter-Reformation had nipped resistance to Rome in the bud, and left independent thinkers to confront her in isolated defiance. The cities which had formerly offered a refuge to Protestant free thought now rigidly formulated their specific creeds, or, like Strasburg, had themselves to submit to the Catholic reaction. Thus it came to pass that these varieties of religious thought found a home on the eastern boundaries of European civilisation, in Poland, where they were welcomed by members of an educated, and to a large extent self-governed, aristocracy. Yet even here, as will be seen, Anti-Trinitarians were carefully excluded from the *Consensus* of Sandomir (1570). Thus was isolated the sect or community associated with the name of Faustus Socinus (1539–1604), like his uncle, Lælius Socinus, a native of Siena and a religious refugee. In Transylvania a Unitarian Church arose about the same time, not, however, organically connected with the Polish 'Socinians.'

<small>Protestant tendencies of Maximilian II.</small> Of course the advocates of Rome laid their finger upon these divisions, and Bellarmine dissected '*Librum quem Lutherani vocant Concordiæ*' in the same year (1586) in which he published the first volume of his chief controversial work. The manifest disunion among the Protestants was the main negative cause of the progress of the Counter-Reformation in this period, and went far to neutralise whatever advantages the Protestant cause might have derived from the accession of Maximilian II. to the imperial throne (1564). During the reign <small>Advance of Protestantism under Ferdinand I.</small> of his father, Ferdinand I. (1558–64), who, Spanish though he was, strove to rule in the interests of peace and unity, the advance of Protestantism throughout the Empire admitted of no doubt. In Franconia, on the Rhine, and

in Westphalia the Reformation progressed; and even the orthodox Duke Albert of Bavaria informed the Pope that a great part of his nobility would rather forego religious worship altogether than return to the Roman rites (1570). The Archbishop of Salzburg told the fathers at Trent (1563) that no power on earth would force many of his subjects to forego their demand for the sacrament in both forms; nor was it till the election of Wolf Dietrich von Raitenau (1590) that the reaction which led to an emigration was here carried out. In Austria no movement has ever so powerfully seized upon both the German and the Slav elements of the population as that of the Reformation; and Ferdinand's home-rule was from the Peace of Augsburg onwards consistently tolerant. In 1564 Pope Pius IV. was as good as his word, and confirmed the concession of the cup which the Estates of Lower Austria had obtained in 1555, and those of Upper Austria in the following year. In Styria, Carinthia, and Carniola, the great majority of the nobility, together with nearly all the burghers of the towns, were Protestants. In Bohemia, where Utraquism was tending to merge into Lutheranism, while the more advanced doctrines of the Bohemian Brethren continued to be widely cherished, Ferdinand I. likewise soon found a policy of mere repression impossible, and in 1564 the Papal concession of the cup to the laity was here also proclaimed. In the Empire at large, where, after a futile religious discussion at Worms (1557), the Diet of Augsburg (1559) had declared its adhesion to the Religious Peace, Ferdinand's government allowed this agreement to be interpreted with considerable laxity, and the notorious "Ecclesiastical Reservation" by which it was accompanied to be treated with scant respect. Protestant administrators enjoyed the revenues of Catholic sees, and a system of imperial "indulgences" even made it occasionally possible for married prelates professing Protestant opinions to sit and vote as spiritual estates at the diet. All this was hard to bear for Ferdinand I.; for although he had long advocated a liberal religious policy at Trent, he was a true Catholic at heart. Thus he fell in with the plan of a gradual recovery of lost ground, and was persuaded to introduce the Jesuits into the Austrian duchies and Bohemia. But the Catholic reaction had not yet taken a firm footing in these countries, when here and in Hungary Maximilian II. succeeded his father as ruler, the remainder of the hereditary dominions being assigned to the two younger brothers.

Maximilian II. (1564–76) played only a negative part towards the religious movement of his age, but this part was by no means without importance. About the year of the religious Peace of Augsburg (1555), the rumours of an inclination on his part towards Protestantism began to take definite shape. The outward conduct of the young King, who was at this time much under the influence of John Sebastian Phauser, a married ecclesiastic, lent colour to the report, and he was denounced to his father by the Jesuit Canisius. Although, notwithstanding his grievances against Spain, he is not known to have interfered with the strictly Catholic life of his Spanish wife, and although he did not withdraw from the observance of the ordinary usages of the Church,

*Negative attitude of Maximilian II. as Emperor.*

he kept away from specifically Catholic solemnities, and insisted on receiving the sacrament in both kinds; while he engaged in the study of Protestant works and in correspondence with Protestants. Every effort was made by Ferdinand I. to turn his son back from the path on which he had obviously entered, though at the same time the Emperor remained deaf to the admonition of Pope Paul IV. (which he had every reason for resenting as well as mistrusting) that he should disinherit his eldest son. Maximilian found himself in a position in which only a heroic type of character would have borne itself with steadfastness. There is no proof that he ever changed his opinions, and some noteworthy evidence to the contrary; but he henceforth outwardly conformed to the Church of Rome, heard orthodox preachers, and even permitted three nuncios in succession—Hosius, Delfius, and Commendone—to prove their zeal by attempts to complete his conversion. Inasmuch as, notwithstanding his declarations, both public and private, the Protestant Electors continued to look forward to his adoption of the Confession of Augsburg after he should have ascended the imperial throne, his election as Roman king in 1562 must be looked upon as the result of an unworthy double game. For Maximilian had now no intention of abandoning either the creed of Rome or the renewed intimate co-operation of the Austrian with the Spanish branch of the House of Habsburg. Dynastic ambition prevailed over all other motives, and just before his father's death Maximilian was in sufficiently good odour of orthodoxy for his claim to the imperial succession to be recognised by the Pope in full consistory.

Thus it came to pass that no such changes as had been at one time anticipated resulted from the accession of Maximilian II. to the imperial throne. While the imperial authority grew weaker and weaker, unstrengthened by any effective foreign policy, which might have shared the glory of Lepanto, or have achieved an earlier Lepanto by land, and while the perverse doctrinal disputes among the Protestants continued, the Catholic propaganda steadily went its way. Maximilian's mind, impatient of nice theological distinctions, and offended by the quarrels of bigotry, seems gradually to have settled itself very near the centre of the balance, though it would be grossly unjust to charge him with religious indifference. Tolerance, in the true sense of the word, was the guiding principle of his conduct. He stood firm against the pressure put upon him by Pope Pius V. to become a persecutor of heretics. On the other hand, he likewise refused the demand of his Austrian Estates for the expulsion of the Jesuits; his business, he told them, was to expel, not the Jesuits, but the Turks. While, however, at the beginning of his reign he had remained in touch with the Protestant interest, he latterly, without abandoning his principle of tolerance, turned in the opposite direction. Spanish marriage schemes, and perhaps speculations on the Polish crown, added their influence, and fears were even entertained that the disappointment caused among the Protestant Estates by the Emperor's bearing might lead to the outbreak of a religious conflict. These fears however proved premature.

In his hereditary dominions, Maximilian, while exacting securities of fair treatment for the Catholics, permitted the Estates of the laity to order the services of the Church in accordance with the Confession of Augsburg. But even in Lower Austria he refrained from establishing a Protestant Consistory under his own headship, and instructed the Lutheran Chytræus, who drew up the service-book both here and in Styria, to include in it as many passages as might be from the Roman ritual. In Austria above the Enns the Estates maintained a more complete religious independence. In Carniola the tide continued in favour of Protestantism for some years beyond the close of Maximilian's reign. In Bohemia, by declaring the Hussite Compactates out of force, he put an end to the established dualism of Catholics and Utraquists, and hastened the amalgamation of the latter with the Lutherans, while the Bohemian Brethren spread more than ever. In Hungary, too, in so far as Maximilian's authority was acknowledged there, Protestantism continued its course unchecked, and deemed itself distinctly countenanced by the King. Among the German temporal princes since the death (1568) of Duke Henry of Brunswick-Wolfenbüttel (Luther's *böser Heinz*), none adhered to Catholicism but Dukes Albert V. (1557–79) and William V. (1579–97) of Bavaria, and, more fitfully, Duke William of Jülich-Cleve-Berg (1539–92). The former, though by no means fanatically disposed (he had obtained the concession of the Cup for his nobility), opened the door to the Catholic Reaction in his dominions; sanctioned the establishment of a very active Index Commission at Munich under the Jesuits Canisius and Peltan (1561), and encouraged the opening of a Jesuit College at Munich (1559), which soon emptied the higher Protestant schools, and of another at Landshut (1578). In the University of Ingolstadt the Jesuits were not established on a solid footing till 1576; but under the bigoted William V. the entire faculty of arts in this university was committed to them *in perpetuum*. The Duke of Cleves, albeit proverbially '*papa in suis terris,*' could not withhold from the greater part of his subjects the desired right of attending Protestant worship. In Würtemberg the ascendancy of the Lutheran clergy and the representatives of the towns in the dominant Committees of the Estates assured the stability of the Reformation. But in the neighbouring Margravate of Baden Catholicism was restored (1570–71) under Margrave Philip, whose father, Philibert, had fallen on the Huguenot side in the battle of Montcontour. (1569). Naturally, however, the regions in which the Counter-Reformation made the most rapid advances were the territories ruled by spiritual potentates. One of the first ecclesiastical magnates to exert himself in that direction was the Abbot of Fulda (Balthazar Gravel), whose six predecessors in succession had allowed the Reformation to spread unhindered among their subjects. Encouraged by Pope Gregory XIII., but appealing, like Albert V. of Bavaria, to the territorial principle established by the Religious Peace, Abbot Balthazar summoned the Jesuits to Fulda, and expelled all the Protestant preachers, together with all the officials, clerical or lay, who refused to accept the Tridentine decrees. Within three years (1573–76) the Catholic

*In the Spiritual Electorates and Principalities.*

restoration in his territories was complete; and a long and bitter conflict, in the course of which he was expelled from his abbacy, ended with his reinstatement and the complete victory of the reaction (1602). The Protestant clergy were likewise driven out of part of the dominions of the Elector of Mainz (the so-called *Eichsfeld*), and Jesuits introduced in their stead, who thence found their way into the diocese of Paderborn and the much-reduced diocese of Hildesheim (1576). In the important Westphalian bishopric of Münster, after two bishops had resigned rather than submit to the Council of Trent, the election of John of Hoya, bishop of Osnabrück (1566), led to the beginnings of a reaction which was arrested by protracted disputes as to his successor's rights (1574 *seqq.*), but resumed after the election to the see of Duke Ernest of Bavaria (1585). Into Würzburg the Jesuits were introduced in 1564, although the intention to connect them with the university (founded 1567) was not carried out till at the time of its second and more enduring foundation by Bishop Julius Echter (1587), when all the chairs of the philosophical faculty were filled by members of the Society. In 1564 Dillingen, the newly-founded University of Augsburg, was completely Jesuitised under Cardinal-Bishop Otto Truchsess, whom Pius IV. had (1560) appointed his *legatus a latere* in Germany; and not long afterwards the Fathers found admission into the free imperial city itself. The bishops of Bamberg and Worms were likewise active in suppressing Protestant worship, and in 1570 the Jesuits entered the Electorate of Treves. Thus in nearly all the 'lands of the crozier' the further reaction of the following reign was prepared under the lax rule of Maximilian II.

All these endeavours glaringly contravened the declaration made by Ferdinand I. at the religious Peace of Augsburg, that there was no desire on the part of the Catholic princes to force their creed upon their Protestant subjects. At the diet which met in 1575 to elect Maximilian's eldest son Roman king, there was, however, a palpable disunion between Lutherans and Calvinists, and the Emperor, keenly alive to the dangers threatening his authority from the increase of the territorial power of the princes by the secularisations, was able to resist the demands of the more active of the Protestants. In his last message to the diet he declared himself to be of no party; but the conditions of the religious conflict were now complicated with foreign alliances and their interests, and thus the germs of the Great War which swallowed up into it all the wars of Europe are already visible during the reign of an Emperor whose heart (be it said to his honour) was from first to last for peace. Rudolf II.

*Progress of the Catholic Reaction in the Empire under Rudolf II.* (1576–1612), who succeeded on the Bohemian and Hungarian as well as on the imperial throne, had not occupied them long before it became apparent that beneath his silent and solitary ways lay concealed a deep religious bigotry, which had been fostered by his early Spanish training. Almost from the outset of his reign (1577) he resided continuously at Prague, while the government of Austria was left in the hands of his brother Ernest, who had been brought up with him in Spain, till the Archduke's death (1595). For the time no attempt was made to touch the privilege of the Austrian nobility of determining for themselves the form of faith they would allow on their own estates; but a strict Catholic uniformity was enforced on the towns, with the result of provoking serious resistance at both Vienna and Linz. In 1578 all persons the orthodoxy of whose religious opinions was doubtful were dismissed from the service of the Court. In Styria Archduke Charles (1564–90), the husband of Maria, sister of Duke Albert V. of Bavaria, in his latter years followed suit, instituting a kind of Catholic visitation throughout his duchy, and admitting into it a Papal nuncio and active sympathisers from Bavaria; but it was not till the actual accession to power (1596) of his son Ferdinand, whom his pious mother would have fain seen a Capuchin friar or a Jesuit father, that religious persecution seems to have begun. Rudolf's own attempts at a Counter-Reformation in Bohemia opened in 1581 with the royal ordinance exiling all the Bohemian Brethren from the realm. The Bohemian nobles were not yet accustomed to receive, much less to obey, commands from their King, and the ordinance remained a dead letter for a full generation (till 1602). The inflictions of Turkish invasion and occupation did not save Hungary from the brutal bigotry of Rudolf, although they deferred its active operations till a comparatively late period of his reign. Meanwhile in the Empire at large the conflict grew more and more acute; nor was it only in the prelatical regions of the Bavarian circle that the Protestants were subjected to a process of extrusion. Unusual interest was excited at the diet, when the Protestant population of historic Aachen defied not only its orthodox town council, but the very imperial army of execution (1581-82). The religious agitation extended along the Rhine, and communicated itself to two cities so different in the character of their religious history as Cologne and Strasburg. In the eyes of pious Catholics no graver scandal had ever been brought upon the Church than that arising out of the conduct of Gebhard II. (of Waldburg-Truchsess), Elector and Archbishop of Cologne (1577-83). Resolved both to marry his mistress and to Protestantise his electorate, he issued an edict (January 1583) granting to his subjects freedom of religious worship, and accomplished the marriage (February). Soon afterwards (April) he was deposed by a Papal bull, and the Catholic majority of the chapter elected his former coadjutor, Ernest of Bavaria, bishop of Lüttich (Liège), archbishop in his stead. Very widespread consequences might have followed, as Ernest was supported by Spanish as well as Bavarian troops, while Henry of Navarre sought to utilise the situation for a Protestant combination. But the Lutheran princes refused to take part in the struggle which ensued, and which did not end till 1589, when Gebhard threw up the game. He now retired to Strasburg, where he was dean. Here the chapter was so hopelessly divided, that on a vacancy in the bishopric in 1592 a schism took place, the Catholic and the Protestant party each choosing a bishop. After a contest of several years, the Catholic bishop (Cardinal of Lorraine) retained the see, and his Protestant rival was compensated in money.

As the reign of Rudolf II. wore on, it seemed for a time as if the Protestant interest would oppose a more united front to the advance of the Catholic Reaction. The successor of Augustus of Saxony, Christian I. (1586–91), was either inclined to Calvinism, or at least he and his Chancellor Krell, as Philippists, objected to the rigour of the *Formula concordiæ*. But the union between Saxony and the Palatinate, where John Casimir, the ally and comrade in arms of the Huguenots, held sway as regent during the earlier years of Frederick IV. (1583–1610), was a mere daydream. In 1591 Christian I. died amidst a storm of religious excitement provoked by his abolition of the exorcistic formula in baptism, to which the great body of his subjects passionately clung; the guardians of his youthful son and successor, Christian II. (1591–1611), proceeded by means of a visitation to uproot Calvinism and Crypto-Calvinism in the electorate, and Krell suffered death. While the two main divisions of Protestantism thus went farther asunder than ever, the Catholic propaganda continued with unabating zeal. In 1590 the Church of Rome made her first convert among reigning Lutheran princes in the person of Margrave James III. of Baden-Hochberg, through the exertions of Pistorius, himself a convert, and afterwards court-preacher to Rudolf II. The joy was great at Rome, where Pope Sixtus V. went on foot to and from the *Te Deum* at Santa Maria de' Tedeschi. As a rule, wherever in this period the Counter-Reformation was at work, the Jesuits were in the van, more especially at the courts and in the sphere of higher education. On the other hand, Rome was during this period not rich in representatives of eminence in popular German polemics, where the bare-footed Franciscan Nasus (Nas), whose chief works were produced about 1570, could hardly be reckoned the equal of the Protestant Fischart.

The Jesuit organisation, which in three provinces (Austria, Upper Germany, and the Rhine) covered nearly the whole of the south and west of the Empire, was likewise strong on its south-western and north-eastern frontiers.

*The Borromean League in Switzerland.*

In 1574 the religious autonomy possessed by the several Swiss cantons enabled the Jesuits to find a welcome at Lucerne, and soon afterwards they reached Freiburg. But the most important Catholic achievement in Switzerland during this period was the conclusion in 1586 of the Golden or Borromean League between the ancient cantons, together with Solothurn and Freiburg, logically followed in the same year by an alliance between these confederates and Spain. The author of the league was the illustrious Archbishop of Milan, who not only established a *Collegium Helveticum* in his cathedral city for the reconversion of Switzerland, but himself laboured actively for the same purpose in the northern districts of his province, which were subject to Swiss cantonal authority. One of the truest representatives of the Counter-Reformation, he consistently combined the persecution of heretics with endeavours at Catholic reform. Inasmuch as the Protestant cantons about the same time united more closely together, especially in view of the danger threatening Geneva from Savoy, the Golden League might have brought about an enduring conflict in the confederation, of which the Mühlhausen troubles (1587) would have been a mere foretaste, had not the failure of the schemes of Philip II. in France and elsewhere gradually inclined the Catholic as well as the Protestant interest in Switzerland to lean upon France; so that the confederation was included in the Peace of Vervins (1598).

In Poland, where the Jesuits were gradually introduced in the latter years of the last representative of the male Jagellon line, Sigismund Augustus (1548–72), they made but little progress during his reign. Before their arrival the Reformation had on the whole steadily advanced, notwithstanding the efforts to the contrary of the Catholic clergy, assisted by the Queen-mother, Bona Sforza (*d.* 1558). While Lutheranism had spread in the towns chiefly inhabited by German settlers, the doctrines of Zwingli and Calvin gained more ground among the nobles, among whom Anti-Trinitarian speculations also largely found admission. After the decrees of the ecclesiastical courts had been deprived of civil effect (1552), full liberty of religious worship was granted to the nobility by another vote of the diet (1556). While in Poland the cry arose for a national synod, which it was hoped would result in the organisation—perhaps under the experienced guidance of the reformer Laski (John a Lasco)—of a national Polish Church, Sigismund Augustus proffered to the Pope demands for concessions similar to those so long urged at Trent by the French and Imperial Governments. The decrees of the council itself, as has been seen, were never accepted by the diet; and in defiance of the labours of Archbishop Hosius, Protes-

*The Catholic Church and the Reformation in Poland.*

tantism continued to flourish in a great variety of forms, Reformed (Helvetian), Bohemian (Waldensian), and Lutheran. In 1570 the Synod of Sandomir at last established that union between the Protestant Churches which had alone seemed wanting for the victory of their cause; but those holding Anti-Trinitarian doctrines were excluded from the '*Consensus*.' It was, then, into so unpromising a field that, after a visit of enquiry by Canisius (1558), Lainez, at the request of Hosius, sent a mission of Jesuit fathers, who established themselves at Braunsberg, and thence, though not favoured by the King, spread over the country at large. On the death of Sigismund Augustus, Henry of Anjou was, after a complicated struggle, elected his successor, the Catholic interest having been at last thrown on his side, largely under the influence of the news of the massacre of St. Bartholomew. The Protestants having, by the 'confederation' adopted by the Diet of Warsaw (January 1573), secured the principle of the religious equality of all the Christian confessions, forced the King before his coronation to swear to maintain the religious liberties of the land. But Henry's word was as water, and during his brief sojourn in Poland the prospects of Rome brightened. After his shameful escape to his new throne in France (1574), another struggle ended in the election of Stephen Bathory, who married the late King's sister, Anna. Like Henry of Navarre, Stephen, in order to secure the crown, allowed himself to be persuaded to profess the Roman faith, though he unhesitatingly confirmed and steadily maintained all the liberties of the Protestant confessions. But with the aid of his consort the Jesuits insinuated themselves into his favour, and during his reign (1576–86) the influence of their order was firmly established in Poland. Their colleges and schools spread over the country, and the King himself set up the central seat of their teaching, the University of Wilna, among a population of which the majority belonged to the Protestant or Greek Churches; while at the University of Cracow, which he opened to all confessions, they contrived to neutralise this liberality. Over the newly created elective judicial tribunals, which were to administer justice to clergy and laity alike, they are likewise said to have established a dominant influence. Stephen Bathory was conscientiously averse to religious persecution, but more especially under the influence of the Jesuit Possevin he allowed the Church of Rome to gain a vantage-ground even in wholly Protestant Livonia, where Jesuit colleges were established at Dorpat and Riga. He even allowed the same influence to affect his foreign policy, and to arrest him in his victorious career against Muscovy, by the treaty of peace negotiated by Possevin (1582).

At the election consequent on Bathory's death, the Protestants by their disunion missed a last opportunity; the Lutherans, in accordance with the intolerant spirit of the age, had already in an early year of his reign (1578) declared against the Union of Sandomir. Purely political considerations led to the election of Sigismund III., son of John of Sweden, who reigned over Poland for forty-five years (1587–1632). Guided by the Jesuits, he pursued a consistent policy against Protestantism, seek-

*The Reformation finally arrested under Sigismund III.*

ing to obtain by corruption what he dared not accomplish by force. The Catholic clergy were encouraged to bring actions at law for the recovery of Church property, and where possible the Catholic worship was restored in edifices which had been appropriated by Protestants. But what was specially characteristic of the reaction in Poland was its worst feature. The mob was repeatedly incited to acts of violence against the Protestants, and prominent among the most infuriated of the fanatics who shared in these manifestations of bigotry and barbarism were the students of Cracow, the pupils of the Jesuits. The Protestants made more than one attempt by themselves (1595), or in combination with the adherents of the Greek Church (1599), to oppose to these proceedings a unity of their own, in which would have lain their best defence. The enlightenment of the country even among Catholics, such as the patriotic Zamoyski (*d.* 1605), was on the side of religious liberty, but its partisans contented themselves with protesting. Thus a new generation grew up, largely, so far as the upper classes were concerned, trained by the Jesuits. Sigismund III., who had formerly lost his Swedish crown for the sake of his faith, in his later years ranged himself and his Polish kingdom against Sweden on the Catholic side in the great European struggle. Poland no longer knew how to control her own destinies; the Counter-Reformation had begun the extinction of a nation.

## CHAPTER V.

### THE RELIGIOUS CONFLICT MERGED IN THE GREAT WAR.

OF the causes contributing to arrest the great religious reaction of the sixteenth century, the most obvious was the failure of Philip II.'s scheme of European policy. The cardinal points of that scheme were the recovery of the Netherlands, the chastisement of England, and the subjection of France. About the beginning of the last decade of the century all these achievements had, humanly speaking, become impossible. In the Netherlands the United Provinces assumed the offensive two years before the efforts of Parma, diverted by Philip's policy and crippled by his jealousy, were quenched in death (1592); and they had practically become an independent power more than half a century before they were acknowledged as such by Spain. As against England and her heretic Queen, though Philip by no means thought to have staked everything upon the Grand Armada, yet with it the moment which seemed his had passed away. The English Government no longer shrank from intervening effectively in France, while with Spain it began to dispute her own ports as well as the waters of the Old World and the

*Failure of the schemes of Philip II.*

*In England and Ireland.*

New. Spain's reprisals in Ireland would have been feeble flashes but for the unspeakable infelicity of England's position between them and native disaffection. Still the prospect of a settlement permitting a free exercise of the Catholic form of faith (1599) passed away as rapidly as it had presented itself. Essex's monstrous blunder only hastened his doom, and the defeat of the hopes founded by many English Catholics upon his wild 'plot' (1601) can hardly be reckoned among Rome's lost opportunities. Hardly better founded were the sanguine expectations which the Catholic, like other interests, persisted in concentrating upon the person of Queen Elizabeth's inevitable successor (1603). It was an age of plots, and upon plots the more active and unscrupulous spirits among the English Roman Catholics had after all to fall back. They profited by neither 'Main' nor 'Bye' (1603), while the discovery of the Gunpowder Plot (1605), and of the acquiescence in it of the head of the Jesuit organisation in England, postponed indefinitely any mitigation of the recusancy laws. The exaction of the oath of allegiance denying the Pope's deposing power (1606) not only extinguished all hopes of the conversion of James I., but induced Pope Paul V. to intervene authoritatively against the acceptance of this test by the English Catholic clergy. The result was a controversy between King James and his apologists on the one side, and the redoubtable Bellarmine (1607–12) on the other, which, like all such controversies, necessarily impeded the propaganda. Such conquests as Catholicism made in England during the next dozen years were made clandestinely and in the teeth of public opinion. Their intrinsic importance was small, though they included Queen Anne; but they helped to show the power of Spain, whose ambassador protected such agents of Rome as Luisa de Carvajal (1613), at the very time when James I. was gratifying popular feeling and his own balancing instincts by marrying his daughter to the 'Palatine.'

The crucial part of the religious conflict in Europe at the beginning of the last decade of the sixteenth century lay in the affairs of France. On the death, twelve days after his election, of Pope Urban VII., the Papal chair was occupied (December 1590) by Gregory XIV. (Sfondrato), who adhered unhesitatingly to the policy of Philip II. and the League. He could not reconcile himself to the accession to the throne of France of 'Vendôme,' as he called Henry IV., and unscrupulously expended the treasure reserved by Sixtus V. for the extreme needs of the Church on the hire of auxiliaries for the cause of orthodox monarchy. This enthusiasm, and the pressure put upon Henry IV. by the *tiers parti* in France to abjure Protestantism, might (1591) have led to the establishment of the French Church as a really independent branch of the Catholic, had it not been for the inability of the Cardinal of Bourbon to assume the office of Patriarch. The interception of Pope Sixtus's letter to Philip II., begging him to relieve Pius and assume the sovereignty (November 1591), completed the unfolding of the situation. Mayenne, who had no desire that the crown should fall to Philip, overthrew the Sixteen, and began to base his calculations on the recognition of Henry IV. In December

*In France.*

1592 Parma died, and the time became ripe for Henry to take the step for which he had long been prepared. Meanwhile, after the brief reign of Innocent IX., Clement VIII. had begun his pontificate (1592–1605). Though no friend of Spain, he at first proceeded cautiously. On the 25th July 1593 Henry IV. formally abjured Protestantism, and the tide of national and anti-Spanish feeling, marked by the publication of the *Satire Menippée*, fully set in. On the 27th February 1594 followed his coronation, which might almost have seemed a defiance of Rome. But though Clement VIII. still hesitated, it was becoming more and more clear to him, as it formerly had to Sixtus V., that France must not be allowed to cut herself adrift from Rome. Unabsolved by the Holy See, Henry of Navarre, in the opinion of both the Sorbonne and the Jesuits, could not claim to be King of France; in the opinion of Jean Chastel, whose design upon Henry's life was discovered in time, he was a tyrant whom it was right to remove. The result was the banishment of the Jesuits from France (1594), which strained the situation still further. Henry IV., who at the beginning of 1595 felt himself strong enough as a national sovereign to declare war against Spain, was at heart anxious to gain the good-will of the Pope; and the Pope in his turn resented the constant pressure upon him of Spanish influence. Curiously enough, the Jesuits, though exiled by Henry IV., showed a sense of favours to come, and some influential members of the order exerted themselves for the absolution of the King. When this was at last granted (17th September 1595), Philip of Spain's hope of mastering France was finally extinguished, and before he died he concluded peace (May 1598). The Edict of Nantes, which shortly before (April) established the rights of the French Protestants on much the same basis as the earlier pacifications obtained and undone in the course of the religious wars, was at first received very wrathfully by Clement VIII., who even threatened to recall his absolution of the King; but the latter took little account of these vapourings, being well aware of the interest which (quite apart from the more special question of its claims on Ferrara) the Papacy had in keeping France strong as against Spain. In the years which followed, Henry IV. on the whole successfully preserved the balance on which his tenure of the throne seemed primarily to depend. His chief councillors were chosen from both sides, a natural preponderance being allowed to the Catholic majority. After a time (1603) he gave his consent to the readmission of the Jesuits into France, and even accepted a Jesuit father as his confessor; nor had the order any corporate or collective responsibility for the crime which put an end to his life. Yet his real sentiments and sympathies remained Protestant to the last, and his foreign policy was only biding its time, and the time of France, who, however marvellous her powers of recuperation, could not be herself again at once. Thus he gradually laid down the lines of that policy by which France ultimately succeeded in overthrowing the predominant influence of the House of Habsburg in Europe; and the House of Habsburg had by this time once more identified itself in both its branches with the cause of Rome.

*System of Henry IV.*

Undoubtedly the Catholic reaction had now more than ever to reckon with an adversary whom a gene-
*Calvinism to the fore.* ration since it had suited Lutheran as well as Catholic statesmanship to ignore. Calvinism, now a militant creed, had determined to bring to an issue the struggle against the common foe, with whom the Lutherans were already again on speaking terms. The centre of these aspirations and schemes was Heidelberg, whence communication was easy to Switzerland, the Netherlands, and France. Here Frederick IV., during the period of his independent government (1592–1610), remained true to the policy of his uncle and guardian, John Casimir. Though himself by no means (except in his potations) an extraordinary man, Frederick IV. fell in with the designs and intrigues of his advisers and agents, among whom Christian I. of Anhalt, himself a convert to Calvinism, was the chief. Between the half-mechanical impetus of the Catholic reaction and the apathy of the Lutherans, they foresaw, and by their efforts helped to make inevitable, the Great War. In this spirit Anhalt conceived and afterwards, though on a much reduced scale, carried into effect, the plan of the Protestant Union.

To this revival of combatant energy in its most determined adversaries the Catholic movement no
*The Counter-Reformation weakened by internal dissensions among the Jesuits. Acquaviva.* longer opposed its former strength and intensity. The very right arm of Rome, the Order of Jesus itself, was lamed by internal dissensions. Already Sixtus V. had cherished projects of reforming the order, and reducing, if not suppressing, its political influence. But

it was in Spain, the true home, as it was the original source, of the order, that its disintegration began. The appointment to the generalship of the Neapolitan Claudio Acquaviva (1581-1615) had excited much discontent among the Spanish Jesuits, who began to think of emancipating themselves in some measure from his control. In return, the general, himself a man in his prime, superseded many of the fathers of more advanced age in the Spanish colleges by younger men, and the consequence was a kind of revolt of the adherents of the *ancien régime*. This movement, led by Henriquez and Mariana, attracted the good-will of Philip II., never at heart a friend of the Jesuits. At Rome, however, the imperturbable Acquaviva obtained from Gregory XIV. (1590-91) a decision against the contentions of the Spanish faction. But under Clement VIII. the Spanish malcontents succeeded in bringing about the summons of a General Congregation of the order as supreme over the general himself (1592); and notwithstanding Acquaviva's success in influencing the results of the discussions of this congregation, he was obliged to submit to an adverse Papal ruling. The effect of these changes was slighter than had been either hoped or feared, but the order inflicted a serious moral loss upon itself by the internal divisions which provoked Pope Clement's reforms of its system. They were followed (1599) by the same Pope's courteous contravention of one of the most cherished principles of the order by pressing the purple upon the great Jesuit controversialist Bellarmine, the first volume of whose *magnum opus* had been placed upon the Index by Sixtus V. because of its refusal to acknowledge the

Pope's immediate lordship over the universe. The death of Clement VIII. (1605) put a term to the attempt, largely inspired by Spain, to undermine the unique position which the Jesuits had hitherto maintained, but the struggle had been severe, and prejudicial to their credit in the Catholic world.

But there was yet another aspect under which the great order seemed, more especially in the judgment of Spaniards, to fall away from its former self-consistency. When, in 1581, Acquaviva authoritatively promulgated the educational course (*Ratio studiorum*) of his Society, and therein showed an evident desire to relieve it from the duty of adhering to pure Thomist dogma, a great shock was given to the conservatism of the schools, and a quarrel prepared itself between Jesuit teaching and the traditions of Spanish theology as especially cherished by the Dominicans. This quarrel came to an outbreak when the Jesuit Molina at Coimbra, in his *Concordia gratiæ et liberi arbitrii* (1588), pushed to an extreme the doctrine of free-will as formulated by the Council of Trent. Other Jesuits wrote about this time on the same subject, but Molina's deductions were the most ambitious and the most complete. The members of the order were by no means unanimous in his favour, but the large majority, including the general, Acquaviva, took his side. As a matter of course the Dominicans began a crusade against Molinism, in which Bannez was their leader; equally of course the Inquisition, now under Manrique, set up its claim to intervene, and a serious crisis seemed imminent in the history of the order. Denounced as heterodox in Spain, the Jesuits

*Molinism.*

gave so much offence in France by their political theories, and the supposed consequences of these for the safety of the sovereign and the welfare of the state, as to be about this time (1594) expelled from the country. Acquaviva accordingly contrived to have the settlement of the controversy removed to Rome itself, where it passed through several interesting and perilous phases, to be finally quashed by Paul V. (1606). Half a century afterwards it was asserted on the one side, but solemnly denied on the other, that this Pope had drawn up a bull in support of the pure Thomistic doctrine.

The political doctrines imputed to the Jesuits excited even more misgivings and mistrust than their specu-lations on the central mystery of moral theology. Lainez had at Trent insisted on the theory, subsequently developed by him in several books, that while the Papacy derives its autho-rity from direct divine institution, the power of princes emanates from, and is therefore in the last resort subject to, the sovereignty of the people. The right of the spiritual authority to bridle the temporal, which Lainez deduced from this contrast between their sources, was extended by Bellarmine to the case of heretic as well as orthodox princes. These principles were consis-tently elaborated in Mariana's book *De rege et regis institutione*, not published till after the accession of Philip III., to whom it was dedicated. As to the re-lations between prince and people, the theory here adopted is the familiar fiction of a contract between them. As to the relations between prince and Church, he is bound to support her privileges, but the Church is not in return bound to bear with him, if, as a tyrant, he

*Jesuit teachings on tyrannicide.*

ruins the commonweal or brings religion into contempt. Should he act thus, the people is entitled in the last resort to treat him as a public enemy, and individual members of the commonwealth may come to the rescue of the whole. Thus Mariana approves of the assassination of Henry III. of France by Jacques Clément, whom he praises as resembling the heroes of antiquity.[1] The substance of Mariana's theory was broached as early as the fifteenth century, when it was explicitly condemned by the Council of Constance. Views not unlike to it were expressed by Calvin, and gained ground accordingly among the French Protestants; while its practical consequences were approved by Pius V. in the case of Ridolfi's plot, and by Sixtus V. in the case of Henry III.'s murder. Moreover, the theory has been denounced by many Jesuit, as it has been held by many non-Jesuit, authorities. Still, the question remains open whether or not Mariana's teaching was in general accordance with the principles of his order, and formed a necessary development of the views of Lainez and Bellarmine. Acquaviva is asserted to have condemned it, but there is a good deal of reservation in his extant declaration; nor in truth could he well have afforded to treat the subject as settled, or have done more than insist (as he did) upon the proper supervision of every doubtful publication on the subject. On the other hand, the elaboration of the doctrine of justifiable tyrannicide indisputably interfered with the progress

---

[1] Clément himself never doubted the intrinsic lawfulness of his deed, though he had scrupled about committing it as a priest; and Ravaillac took up much the same ground in stating his motives for taking vengeance on Henry IV.

of the Catholic reaction in countries where a Protestant, or a Catholic suspected of Protestant leanings, sat on the throne. In France, Mariana's book was prohibited by the Parliament of Paris after Henry's murder (1610), though the Queen Regent suspended the decree. In England the enforcement of the oath denying the Pope's right to authorise the deposition of kings led to a split among the Roman Catholic clergy, to which Paul V. sought to put an end by a declaratory brief (1606). After (in 1610) Bellarmine had fully elaborated the conclusion that the Pope possesses the power of releasing the subjects of temporal princes from their allegiance and transferring it to some other quarter, King James I. himself descended into the arena. One thing at least was clearly demonstrated by the famous controversy which ensued, viz., Rome's real want of foothold in England, notwithstanding all the efforts of the advanced guard of the Papacy. It may be noticed in passing that Clement VIII. in 1599 declined to entertain a proposition for the canonisation of Ignatius Loyola.

But the Papacy itself seemed no longer able to sustain the movement of the Counter-Reformation at its previous height. Clement VIII. (1592–1605) was by no means unsuccessful in his praiseworthy attempts at 'making peace between the kings' (Vervins, 1598); but he was content with adjusting where his predecessors would have claimed to arbitrate. In matters religious, he sought to maintain the purity of the faith by the customary methods; the Inquisition was by no means inactive at Rome during his reign, and immolated a

*Decline of the reforming spirit at Rome. Clement VIII.*

few heretics, one of whom, as it seems no longer possible to doubt, was Giordano Bruno. But under Clement VIII. a lower tone once more begins to characterise the whole system of government and life at Rome, though he did what he could to maintain some of the reforms of Sixtus V. The Vatican swarmed with *nepoti*, and nearly two-thirds of the Sacred College were pensioners of foreign courts. Well pleased with an acquisition long coveted by the Papacy—that of Ferrara (1598)—Clement in his later years, when the great jubilee of 1600 lay behind him, showed little disposition to carry on the religious movement aggressively. He refused to have any part in the attempt of Charles Emmanuel of Savoy to "escalade" Geneva, the citadel of Calvinism (1601), and in vain exhorted the English Catholics, rendered desperate by apparently interminable injustice, to refrain from such remedies as sedition and conspiracy (1604). Yet when, after the brief pontificate of Leo XI. (Medici), Paul V. (Borghese) was seated in St. Peter's chair (1605-21), a change seemed once more to come over the spirit of the Papacy. The new Pope seemed as it were transformed by his election, in which, having contributed nothing to the result himself, he saw the finger of God bidding him follow the examples of the most conscientious and the most zealous among his predecessors. Nor should it be forgotten how mighty a position the Church of Rome now occupied through the successful activity of the Catholic, and more especially of the Jesuit, missions in the New World, and in the remotest regions of the Old—in the East Indies, China, and Japan. At the very time

<small>Revival under Paul V.</small>

when in Europe Catholicism was preparing for a final struggle against the Protestant revolt, the idea arose of a reunion under the Papal supremacy of a whole series of Eastern Churches between the Indus and Euphrates with the Church of Rome; and to this lofty dream neither Philip III. of Spain nor Paul V. himself remained strangers.

At home, Paul V. consistently, though without harshness, exacted from both bishops and clergy a rigorous fulfilment of their duties. At the same time, without shaping his foreign policy in subservience to either France or Spain, he set about the restoration of the authority of the Church where it seemed to have been impaired, beginning with certain ecclesiastical grievances in Spain and in Genoa. These successes increased his ambition to an extraordinary degree, and before the first year of his pontificate was ended he had become involved in a serious quarrel with the Republic of Venice, which had recently re-enacted, together with a kind of mortmain statute, a law requiring the assent of the temporal authorities to the opening of new churches, and had asserted the jurisdiction of the state over criminous ecclesiastics. Paul V. replied to these rather high-handed proceedings by threatening to place Venice under an interdict, unless within twenty-seven days these laws were repealed and the imprisoned ecclesiastics given up (April 1606). Venice, not for the first time in her history exposed to the Papal thunder, stood firm; and the interdict descended upon Doge, Seigniory, and city. The clergy, under the orders of the State, continued to perform

*Paul V.'s quarrel with Venice.*

their spiritual functions, and to administer the sacraments; where there was hesitation, more or less of pressure was effectually applied; and the Jesuits, who refused submission to the civil authorities, were summarily expelled from the territories of the Republic. Hereupon the literary champions of Rome, headed of course by the Jesuits, set in scene a futile blaze of indignation, in which, after the efforts of their Bergamesque printing-press had been met by the great Venetian publicist and patriot Fra Paolo Sarpi, Cardinal Bellarmine himself took part. But it did not suit Henry IV. of France to allow the conflict with Spain to break out on this issue, for he had no wish that the good-will of the Pope should be secured to Spain beforehand; moreover, Spain herself was too much impoverished to be willing to enter suddenly into war. Thus through the mediation of Cardinal Joyeuse a pacification was patched up between the Pope and Venice (1607). The imprisoned clerics were indirectly given up to the Pope, and a semblance of absolution was supposed to have been pronounced, but the obnoxious laws were not repealed, nor were the Jesuits recalled for half a century to come. The weakness of the Papal authority even on the Italian side of the Alps had been unmistakably exposed, and rumour represented Rome as reduced to employing the assassin's dagger by way of counter-argument to the State theology of Venice. What if the Republic, still a great name, if no longer a great power, were, under Sarpi's guidance, altogether to throw off its allegiance to the Church and to become Protestant? Such thoughts accorded only too well with the eager aspirations of eager Protestants like the Huguenot Duplessis-Mornay and his friend Sir Henry Wootton, the diplomatic agent of England at Venice; nor probably was Fra Paolo's own attitude on the subject of a purely negative character. But it was again Henry IV. who declined to hasten a disruption of the Church in Italy, and preferred tentatively to resume his scheme of a union of the Italian states. Paul V., though his reign lasted for nearly fourteen years longer, never again allowed his zeal to outrun his discretion, as it had in the Venetian imbroglio. He maintained the Papal claims in theory, and humoured the Jesuits in their theological controversy with the Dominicans; but the spirit of combat had passed out of him, and instead of re-establishing the Papal supremacy in Europe, or even in Italy, he founded the fame of the Borghese family as the most splendid patrons of art at Rome.

Enfeebled at its centre, the movement of the Catholic Reaction still seemed in more remote regions to follow a well-established *impetus*. This was the period in which the Catholic Church regained her ascendancy in Poland under Sigismund III., in which the same prince, 'with the same thorn in his foot' (Malaspina), sought to reintroduce Catholicism into Sweden, in which Rome and her Jesuit vanguard actually founded hopes upon the enterprise of the first false Demetrius in Russia (1605-6). But these were merely operations on the outskirts. After the overthrow of the great plan of Philip II., it seemed for a time as if the renewal of the religious conflict must inevitably take the shape of an assault upon the European ascendancy of the House of

*Catholic advances in Poland and Russia.*

Habsburg under the leadership of Henry IV. of France, the last, and not the least successful, of Philip's adversaries. But Henry was determined before and above everything to rally the whole French nation round his throne, and to effect this, even at the risk of offending his old Huguenot associates and disappointing his most trusted counsellors, he made concession upon concession to the Church of Rome. His marriage with Maria de' Medici (1600) was followed by the recall of the Jesuits into France (1604), and no obstacle was placed by his government in the way of a religious movement which recalls some of the most attractive features of the earlier stages of the Counter-Reformation. Great activity manifested itself in the religious orders of both sexes, many of which were reformed, largely under the influence of the Spanish movement identified with the name of St. Teresa, some putting out fresh shoots, as did the Cistercians in the *Feuillants*, who were ultimately, under Clement VIII., constituted a distinct order. No name was more prominent in these endeavours than that of François de Sales, afterwards canonised (1567–1622), a mystic with whom fervour of feeling took the place of subtlety, and perhaps of depth, of thought. In conjunction with the pious Baroness de Chantal he founded the female order of the Visitantines (1610), modelled on that of the Ursulines, which had come into France from Italy, where it had flourished under the protection of Cardinal Borromeo. François de Sales, when charged with the task of re-Catholicising the district of Chablais, of which Charles Emmanuel of Savoy had in 1594 despoiled the Genevese, had displayed extraordinary energy;

being credited in a Papal bull with having made 72,000 converts; and in 1602 he had been appointed Bishop of Geneva *in partibus*. Of hardly less importance were the labours of Vincent de Paula, a native of Gascony (1576–1660), the founder of the Priests of the Mission (confirmed by Louis XIII. in 1627, and by Urban VIII. in 1631), afterwards, from the great Paris priory assigned to their use, known as the Lazarists, and, in conjunction with Louise de Gras, of the Sisters of Charity known as the Grey Sisters (1634). He had been introduced to the sphere of home missionary work, in which he accomplished so much, by Pierre de Berulle, a kind of intermediary between France and Spain in the work of the great Theresian reform. Henry IV. was thus pursuing a cautious religious policy at home, but continuing at the same time to carry on his designs for the extension of the influence of France both in Italy and among the German Protestants, whose Union (1608) was greatly in his favour, when his career was cut short by the knife of the *Feuillant* Ravaillac (May 14, 1610). His widow, Maria de' Medici, now Regent of France, did her best to preserve the public peace; but the principle of national unity represented by Henry suffered very palpably by his death. The great Huguenot lords began to claim extended securities, and the Guises once more sought to lay hands upon the helm. The double marriage treaty with Spain (1612) implied a Catholic political alliance; once more monarchical and clerical ideas and interests were in unison, while the Sorbonne, led by Edmund Richer, strove to uphold the liberties of the Gallican Church. No alliance was, however, effected between the national section of the clergy and the Huguenots, who relied chiefly on the heads of the great houses (Bouillon, Rohan, Soubise, Sully), and were by them once more carried in the direction of that aristocratic decentralisation, which under Henry IV. the genius of France seemed to have abandoned.

The course of religious affairs under Henry IV. in France had reacted upon Switzerland, where Catholics and Protestants were far more evenly balanced. The Catholic propaganda had been active at Lucerne, and a Spanish party formed itself in several of the Cantons. But it was in the Catholic district of the Valtelline, over which the Protestant canton of the Grisons held sway, that an imminently dangerous complication arose. Henry IV.'s overtures to the Grisons, about the time of his alliance with Venice (1603), were answered by the construction of a Spanish fortress (F. Fuentes) in the Milanese, hard by their frontier, and the eastern passes of the Alps seemed in question. But when, after the death of Henry IV., French policy changed, the Catholic interest in Switzerland felt reassured, and Spain secured to herself by a brutal massacre the control of the Valtelline (1620); nor was it till many years later (1635), when Richelieu had resumed the policy of Henry IV., that the Spanish and Imperial troops were again ejected from this important valley.

*Catholic revival in Switzerland.*

But it was in Germany and in the kingdoms ruled by the Austrian branch of the House of Habsburg that the relations between the confessions had long been such as to make the open

*The Reaction under Rudolf II.*

outbreak of the conflict a mere question of time and opportunity. As the reign of Rudolf II. proceeded, his Spanish bigotry continued to make itself felt as unmistakably as his political incompetence. He was unmarried, but his brothers, Archdukes Ernest and Albert, were successively connected with the Spanish government and policy. Of his sisters, one was the mother of Philip III., and another died as a nun in Spain. Of Archduke Matthias alone, after his brother Ernest's death (1595) Rudolf's probable successsor, nothing could be predicted as to his religious or general policy, except that it would be always dictated by his immediate personal interests. Of the side-lines of the House of Austria, the Styrian alone survived in numerous scions, of whom the head was Archduke Ferdinand. He had succeeded his father as a boy of twelve years of age; and to him, owing to the childlessness or celibacy of the princes of the main line, a strong and widespread interest began to attach itself. When in 1596 he took the administration of his archduchy into his own hands, he at once began the experiment which at a later date and on a larger scale he put into practice in Bohemia. All Protestant worship was prohibited; all Protestant schools were closed; all Protestant preachers banished under pain of death; while to the laity was left the choice between conversion and exile, accompanied by harsh conditions as to the disposal of property. The peasantry came in swarms to be converted before soldiers were quartered upon them; but though the pressure applied was assuredly severe, even the Styrian Counter-Reformation only partially accomplished its work. In

*Ferdinand of Styria.*

1609 Ferdinand is found replying to a 'renewed application' of the nobility and peasantry of Styria, Carinthia, and Carniola for the free exercise of the Augsburg Confession. Rudolf's own attempts at a Counter-Reformation in his favourite Bohemia began to take practical effect when, in 1602, Jesuit, Capuchin, and cognate influences prevailed upon him, by reviving and extending the operation of an ordinance promulgated in 1581, to deprive Lutherans, Calvinists, and Bohemian Brethren alike of a settled religious status. Much persecution and hardship ensued, including the suppression of the Carmel of the Bohemian Brethren at Jungbunzlau; while the majority of the diet resented the acceptance of the Trent decrees by a Catholic synod, and their enforcement by the Archbishop of Prague. These feelings were intensified by the proceedings of Rudolf's government in Hungary, where, in the parts of the kingdom unoccupied by the Turks, religious persecution was now added to a contemptuous neglect of the national laws and usages. This policy bore its fruit when Stephen Bocskai, after invading the country (1604), was by a numerous diet proclaimed ruler of Hungary and Transylvania (1605). In order to be able to conclude peace with the Turks, Matthias, as the representative of Rudolf (though anything but trusted by him), listened to Stephen Illeshazi and the other Magyar nobles (1606), and afterwards confirmed the code of laws in which the concession of free religious worship to both Lutherans and Calvinists had been incorporated (1608).

Outside the Austrian dominions the best ally of the Roman reaction had long been the incurable disunion among the Protestants. The endeavours of the Elector Palatine Frederick IV. (from 1594 onwards) had been wrecked upon the refusal of the Saxon Government to co-operate with him, and the reaction seemed to be left without a check.

*Protestantism persecuted and blocked in the Empire.*

This was the time of the first efforts of Duke Maximilian of Bavaria (1597–1651), afterwards called Max the Catholic, and almost as important a factor in the great Catholic effort of his age as Ferdinand II. himself, to whom he stood successively in the relations of brother and son-in-law. As the new century opened, the endeavours of the spiritual princes to bring their stray subjects back into the fold became more and more alarming. In the three spiritual electorates, and in other sees, such as Paderborn in especial (where Bishop Theodore of Fürstenberg in 1604 issued forth completely victorious from a desperate struggle with his nobility and burghers), an era of unrelenting intolerance set in. Yet while beyond the frontiers of the Empire allies were on all sides proffering themselves to the Protestant cause, no Protestant grievance had a chance of being listened to at the diet, and in the supreme court of appeal (*Reichskammergericht*) all decisions of cases turning on the disputed points in the religious Peace of Augsburg were as a matter of course against the Protestants. Secession from the nexus of the Empire being regarded as out of question, the sole expedient left was that of the union *in imperio* which had so repeatedly been essayed in vain. Saxony under Christian II., and under his successor, John George I. (1611–56), whose counsels were inspired by the court preacher Hoë von Hoënegg, still refused to dally with Calvinism; but in Brandenburg the latter form of Protestantism was in the ascendant under Joachim Frederick (1598–1608), and actually established (1614) under John Sigismund (1608–19). Brunswick, Hesse-Cassel, Baden, and Anhalt were likewise more or less favourable to a scheme of confederation; Würtemberg too was gained over, and it was chiefly the quarrel of Henry IV. with the Huguenot Duke of Bouillon which for a time foiled the indefatigable efforts of Prince Christian of Anhalt, the agent-in-chief of the Palatine policy. Thus it was not till the critical year 1606 that an event happened which was to lead to the accomplishment of his design. The Emperor Rudolf's mania had now reached such a pitch, and the impotence of his rule exhibited so shameful a contrast with the severity of his ordinances, especially in matters of religion, that it seemed time to deprive him of at least the reality of monarchical authority. Archduke Matthias hereupon completely identified himself with the Hungarian demands, while in Transylvania, where, after a brief interval, Gabriel Báthory had succeeded Bocskay (1608), the Catholics, and the Jesuits in particular, had now in their turn to undergo persecution. Meanwhile, regardless of the counsels of either friend or foe, with neither reason to steady nor religion to console him, Rudolf was sinking deeper and deeper; and whatever power remained to him in any of his dominions would clearly soon slip away from his weakly grasp.

*The Palatine policy of aggression.*

When the Palatine policy, embodied in Christian of Anhalt, was straining every nerve to bring about, in co-operation with the foreign enemies of the house, the overthrow of the Austrian Habsburgs and the ruin of the Church of Rome, in so far as these two objects were inseparable from one another, a pretext for action was sure to be found before long. It was furnished by the proceedings at Donauwörth, where a riot consequent upon attempts at a Counter-Reformation, instigated by the Duke of Bavaria and the Bishop of Augsburg, had led to the city being first placed under the ban of the Empire, and then left in the hands of Maximilian, who, with Jesuit aid, now attempted a thorough restoration of Catholicism in the city (1607). Early in the following year the issue decided itself between Rudolf and Matthias, who, besides being now at the head of the national party in Hungary, had tampered with the loyalty of the Austrian Estates, his efforts being seconded by Bishop Khlesl of Vienna, a bigot, but, as a pupil of the Jesuits, ready to take the side on which most could be done for the glory of God. As in Moravia, too, Matthias found support, an agreement was, with the aid of Philip III. of Spain and Pope Paul V., at last (June 1608) forced upon Rudolf, whereby he resigned to Matthias Hungary, Austria, and (for his lifetime) Moravia, retaining with the imperial crown Bohemia, where, however, Matthias was to succeed him, and the Catholic Tyrol. This partial victory of Matthias was one of neither creed nor principle, but it gave a tremendous shock to the imperial authority, and added enormously to the self-consciousness of the Protestant Estates, by means of whom Matthias had climbed into power. Taken together with the loss suffered by the Protestant cause at Donauwörth, these proceedings could not fail to impress upon Christian of Anhalt the necessity for immediate action. Thus, even before the Habsburg compact was sealed, the Protestant Union was concluded at Ahausen (May 1608). Though the number of its members rapidly grew, Anhalt's proposal to extend it to the hereditary dominions of the House of Austria was thought too daring, and Henry IV. delayed to signify his adhesion. Meanwhile Matthias, though desirous of remaining on amicable terms with Spain and Rome, found himself obliged still further to conciliate Protestant feeling in Austria, while in Hungary he was king in little more than name. About the same time in Bohemia Rudolf in his turn was constrained by the Protestant majority, both inside and outside the diet, to grant the famous *Letter of Majesty* (July 1609), which, while restricting the right of building churches or schools to certain of the Estates, gave to all inhabitants of Bohemia absolute freedom of choice between the Catholic faith and the Confession of Augsburg. There was joy at these successes among the opponents of Rome, from Christian of Anhalt to Fra Paolo, but the victory was anything but assured; and two days before the signature of the Letter of Majesty at Prague the Catholic League had been founded at Munich. Yet, although the recent death of Duke John William of Juliers-Cleves-Berg had, by reason of the local situation of the disputed territories, opened a succession question likely at last to set Europe in flames, and although the Union was prepared to take every advantage of the difficulty, the time had passed

*Establishment of the Protestant Union.*

*And of the Catholic League.*

for a cordial co-operation between the Catholic powers, such as the Guises had striven to bring about half a century before. Even the Pope hesitated, but Philip III. of Spain became Protector of the League, which by the summer of 1610 included nearly all the more important Catholic princes of the Empire. A few months earlier (February 1610) the high-handed occupation of Juliers by the Archduke Leopold had at last clinched the alliance between the Union and Henry IV., who immediately entered into effective negotiations with Savoy, the United Provinces, and James I. of England. The Scandinavian powers were friendly, and when early in May Henry announced that he found himself under the necessity of marching through the Spanish Netherlands in order to assist his ancient allies in the disputed Duchies, he had virtually a confederation of Protestant Europe at his back. His assassination once more postponed what had now seemed the inevitable outbreak of the great religious conflict. While the Juliers dispute dragged its slow length along, the question of the succession to Matthias, who took Rudolf's place on the imperial throne (1612), after ousting him (1611) from the Bohemian, became paramount. The choice of Ferdinand of Styria as the future head of the House of Austria implied a policy of combat against the Union as well as against Protestant claims at home. For such a struggle, however, Matthias made no preparation, allowing Bethlen Gabor to seat himself firmly on the Transylvanian throne (1613–15), and thus establish a firm anchorage for Protestantism on the Bohemian frontier. Yet soon afterwards permitting the flat violation of the Letter of Majesty in Bohemia itself (1616), and inducing the diet at Prague to recognise Ferdinand as his successor. There only remained, when the time should come, the imperial election, at which the opposition of the Palatine policy would have to be overcome. The new head of the Palatine house, the young Elector Frederick V. (from 1610), was the son-in-law of James I. of England, with whom (1612), as with the United Provinces (1613–14), the Union had concluded treaties of alliance. But its strength was apparent rather than real, as was shown by the indecisiveness of its action in the Duchies, and by the hesitation of its members, when the time of its formal expiration drew near, to bind themselves for a longer period than three years.

Like Henry III. of France, Matthias at this time (1617) stood helpless against the association of the two Confessions in the Empire, and utterly impotent against the forces which they, though inadequately, represented. The collision between these two forces, though postponed by policy, by half-heartedness, and by apprehensions which the event justified a hundredfold, was no longer to be avoided. And such, notwithstanding many failures and reverses, had been the persistent and indefatigable activity of the Counter-Reformation movement—such, too, had been the caprices of fortune, which had substituted James I. for Henry IV., and was about to substitute Ferdinand II. for Matthias, that the case of the Reaction was now anything but hopeless. France and Spain were at peace with one another, and the religious policy of the former State was rapidly reassimilating itself to that

*Imminence of the great conflict of the Confessions.*

*The Catholic prospects of success.*

traditional to the House of Habsburg. Indeed, the decree which in 1617 ordered the restoration of the Church estates in Béarn was an anticipation in small of the Edict of Restitution. Again, the spiritual head of the Catholic world, Paul V., in his later years anxiously strove to avert anything that might impair its unity, through which, in the earlier years of his reign, his arrogance had threatened to make a breach. Moreover, Philip III. of Spain had been by his Minister Lerma brought to perceive that the day had passed for aiming at a hegemony over Western and Central Europe, although king and people still believed in the mission of Spain as the foremost of the Catholic powers. At home, the Inquisition maintained its authority, and asserted it by such acts as the expulsion of the Moors from Spain (1609); and at no time has the influence of the Church over the minds of men been more visibly omnipotent in Spain than in the early half of the seventeenth century, the period of the *comedias de santos* and *autos sacramentales* of Lope, Calderon, and their contemporaries. Abroad, the Spanish Government had for some time carried on a propaganda alternating between conversion and corruption, directed to the courts rather than to the peoples, which was no altogether ineffective preparation for the resumption of more direct efforts for the aggrandisement of the power of Spain and Rome. Among the German Habsburgs the miserable *Bruderzwist* was at an end, and the day was soon at hand when they would acknowledge as their head the most unflinchingly orthodox of their number, Ferdinand II., intimately allied by marriage and in religious policy with Maximilian of

Bavaria, the head of the Catholic League, and the chief potentate of the German South-West. Even in the North and East there was some reason for hopefulness. The orthodox Sigismund of Poland had never abandoned his claims to the Swedish throne, and was about to make war on its Protestant occupant, Gustavus Adolphus. In Denmark the signs of a Catholic reaction were still few and scant, but the Danish Princess Anne, who shared the English and Scottish thrones, and whose sister Hedwig was about this time suggested as a consort for Ferdinand of Styria, had become a secret convert to Rome. Nor was the day distant when further efforts would be made towards the recovery of England for Rome, less direct, but hardly less alarming to Protestant popular sentiment, than those devised by Philip II. In the meantime, the influence of Spain had never been more in the ascendant with the English court and Government than now; the Spanish marriage negotiations were uppermost in the mind of James I., and in 1618 he sacrificed Raleigh to the demands of Gondomar. The Protestants, on the other hand, entered into the struggle disunited, and for the most part dispirited. They were without a leader, except the youthful Elector Palatine, Frederick V. France seemed lost as an ally, and England hopeless. Never had the religious controversies between the several Protestant parties and sects been more bitter. The Synod of Dort met in the very year in which the Great War broke out (1618). Never had the labour expended, especially among the Calvinists, upon the compilation of vast and provocative bodies of theological doctrine been more intense.

*Their superiority to the Protestant chances.*

In some quarters the democratic tendencies of advanced Protestantism were alarming conservative sympathies; elsewhere its increasing narrowness was estranging cultivated minds.

No attempt can be made here to narrate the course of the struggle, which opened thus far from unfavourably for the cause of the Catholic Reaction. There were stages in the progress of the Thirty Years' War (1618—1648) when that movement seemed on the eve of more notable advances than any which have been recorded in the course of this sketch. The one enduring gain of the Counter-Reformation was the recovery by Rome of Bohemia, where she had lost her supremacy for the better part of two centuries. This gain would have undoubtedly been far more extensive had it not been for the sagacious vigilance and untiring energy of the Prince of Transylvania, Bethlen Gabor (1613–29). In his endeavours to hold the balance between that house and the Turk, he naturally availed himself of the Protestant feeling in Hungary and in the hereditary dominions of the House of Austria: his own temperament inclined towards tolerance rather than confessional enthusiasm. Protestantism contrived to maintain itself in Hungary throughout the reign of Ferdinand II. (1619–37), and after the pressure of his and his adviser Cardinal Pázmány's Catholic zeal had been removed, George Rákóczy's insurrection led to a fairly satisfactory settlement of the Protestant grievances and demands (1645–46).

The history of the Counter-Reformation, and that of movements analogous to it, hardly contain a second passage resembling the record of the restoration of Catholicism in Bohemia. After the so-called Bohemian War had come to an end with the battle of the White Hill at Prague (November 8, 1620) and the flight of Frederick, Bohemia lay at Ferdinand's mercy, and by the spring of 1621 his authority was restored throughout his dominions. With his measures of political punishment and retaliation in Bohemia, Silesia and Moravia, and in Upper Austria, we cannot here concern ourselves. The religious reaction began at Prague so soon as King Frederick and his caravan had turned their backs on the city gates. It continued to rise even after (February 1622) a general pardon had been issued. It was still in progress when, after the first great victory of Gustavus Adolphus, the Elector John George invaded Bohemia as the ally of the Swedish deliverer (1631); and its operations were by no means at an end with the Peace of Westphalia (1651 was a notable year of emigrations). The general direction of the proceedings was entrusted to the governor of Bohemia, Prince Charles of Liechtenstein, and to the Archbishop of Prague, Ernest von Harrach; while under them the chief management fell to Count Paul Michna, a pupil of the Jesuits, who had formerly, as secretary of the kingdom, countersigned the Letter of Majesty. Their joint action was characterised by that species of deliberation which is best calculated to ensure completeness. On the closing, destruction, or reconsecration of Protestant churches followed the expulsion, in succession, of the clergy of the Bohemian Brethren, of the Calvinists, of the Bohemian (Utraquist), and finally of

*The Bohemian Counter-Reformation.*

the German, Lutherans. Commissaries, at times with troops of dragoons at their back, effected this with often brutal rigour. By Ferdinand's wish they were, when possible, accompanied by Jesuits, so that no opportunity might be lost of converting the inhabitants. Jesuits and Dominicans took the places of the expelled ministers. In Prague, Olmütz, and Breslau, and in other towns of Bohemia and the dependant provinces, the Jesuits assumed a complete command of higher and secondary education; but in the villages ignorant Polish monks had often to be put in the vacant incumbencies, or there was for a time a complete *solitudo clericorum*. As a matter of course, a raid was made on all heretical books, especially on German and Bohemian Bibles,—indeed, to make sure, upon all Bohemian books whatever. Within about fifteen years Catholic uniformity was re-established in Bohemia; but the forced emigrations of recusants, which had begun in 1622, continued after the victory had been outwardly consummated. In 1627 a royal patent of reformation offered to the Protestant nobility the choice between conversion and banishment, and the majority preferred the latter alternative. A vast transfer of estates followed. Nor was it only among the nobles and in the towns that a steadfast spirit was displayed, as is shown by some noteworthy peasants' revolts. Though it should be remembered to the honour of Ferdinand II. that he explicitly desired the restoration of religious unity to be unstained by bloodshed, yet the thoroughness of the Bohemian Counter-Reformation remains without a parallel; for it involved a denationalisation of the government and official administration, of the educational system, and to some extent of the very literature and language of the land. In the dependant countries, Moravia and Silesia, similar measures had similar results. In Upper Austria, the Counter-Reformation began with an expulsion *en masse* of 'Anabaptists.' After the Protestant invasions and peasants' rebellions which ensued the work thus begun was accomplished, as was believed, to the extent of the complete extinction of Protestantism (1628). In Lower Austria the procedure was much the same, though to the nobility more consideration was here shown, and the propaganda had to content itself with a more gradual advance. When, in 1623, the Palatine Electorate, forfeited by the unfortunate Frederick V., was formally bestowed upon Maximilian of Bavaria, the prospect opened of yet another German land being brought back to the fold by a similar series of operations.[1] At the close of the first period of the Thirty Years' War (1624 c.), the progress of the Catholic Reaction seemed assured, if the Emperor maintained his ascendancy in Germany, which he had established with the aid of Spain and the League; and, secondly, if the good understanding between Spain and France endured. The accession to the Papacy, early in the course of the Great War, of Gregory XV. (1621–23), had contributed to strengthen the cause of Rome. Though an old and broken man, who left the entire management of his affairs to Cardinal Lodovisio and

<small>The Counter-Reformation in Austria;</small>

<small>And in the Palatinate.</small>

---

[1] The Nuncio Caraffa at Vienna thus succinctly summarised the normal process of counter-reformation: *Primo diligens instructio seductorum; deinde minæ, propositio immunitatis, præposita præmia; denique obstinatorum ejectio.*

his other *nepoti*, he pursued a rigidly orthodox policy, and exhibited a devotion to Spain unknown at the Vatican since the days of Clement VIII. Gregory XV. was succeeded by Urban VIII. (1623–44). So far as the advancement of his family (the Barbarini) was concerned, the new Pope followed in the footsteps of his predecessor; but his policy was peculiar to himself. True, Urban was in principle as consistent an adversary of Protestantism, and as alive to the importance of Catholic effort, as were any of the Popes of the Counter-Reformation. If Gregory XV. had canonised Ignatius Loyola, he canonised Francis Borgia. In 1627, at the very time of the triumph of the Emperor, he renewed the bull *In cœnâ Domini*, and he symbolised its claims by a monument in St. Peter's to the Countess Matilda. But he hereby likewise expressed his defiance of the imperial authority, and emphasised his determination to treat the Great War not as a religious conflict, but as turning on the political relations between the powers. He accordingly viewed with undisguised displeasure the overwhelming coalition of Spain and Austria, encouraged the efforts of France to recover her influence in Italy, and at least did nothing to hinder the victorious progress of Gustavus Adolphus and of the Protestant cause.

During the earlier years, however, of Urban VIII.'s papacy, the advance of the Catholic Reaction knew no break; and the results of the so-called Danish war (1625–29) were such as to suggest an attempt to undo on a large scale the compromise of the religious Peace of Augsburg. Christian IV. of Denmark had been unwillingly left in the lurch both by Charles I. of England and by Richelieu. The relations between King Charles and his Parliament made it impossible for him to transmit more than a fraction of the promised subsidies. As for Richelieu, who since 1624 stood at the head of affairs in France, though the French Government had taken serious note of the great increase of power which had accrued to the House of Habsburg from the results of the Bohemian and Palatinate wars, he was first hampered by the aggressive movements of the Huguenots, and then derided for having offered them a conciliatory settlement (1625). Thus he had to allow the Danish War to take its course, and even to compromise the Valtelline question, in which his *coup de main* had intervened, by the Peace of Monçon (March 1626). France seemed less likely than ever to oppose the cause of Habsburg and Rome, when the great plot was formed against Richelieu (1625–26), and when the war against the Huguenots, in which Buckingham's ambition had led to the futile intervention of England, ended with the fall of Rochelle (1627–28). For the moment it might even seem as if a complete Catholic restoration were possible in France. But Richelieu, whose hand grew firmer and firmer on the helm, was far removed from any such intention. He granted moderate terms to the Huguenots in the Edict of Nîmes (1629), and made peace with England (1630). His desire was to resume the contest with Spain, and for this the question of the Mantuan succession soon furnished him with the desired opportunity.

The complete triumph in the Danish War of the armies of Emperor and League, which were overrunning the whole of Lower Saxony, over the first substantial Protestant combination which had yet been formed, intoxicated the Catholic world with joy. Even Pope Urban VIII. took up the notion, which both Olivarez and Richelieu pretended to favour, of a new Grand Armada against Protestant England, poor Queen Anne being assigned the part of a kind of latter-day Mary Queen of Scots. The air was full of other visionary schemes; and although the arrogance of Wallenstein was defied by the walls of Stralsund, never had the power of the house of Habsburg been more imposing, or its exertions on behalf of the Catholic Reaction more varied. Ferdinand II. had armies in the field in the Low Countries, in Poland, and before Mantua; and soon Pope Urban VIII. must have consented to crown him Roman Emperor on Italian soil. And rather more than two months before concluding peace with his vanquished adversaries at Lübeck (May 1629) he promulgated that Edict of Restitution which sought to carry back the religious history of the Empire more than seventy years. Afterwards, when the Edict of Restitution had proved to have been a fatal blunder, it was declared to have been inspired by the craft of Richelieu. In truth, it originated in the desire expressed at Mühlhausen (1627) by the members of the League, and by the spiritual electors in particular, that all Catholic complaints as to violations of the *reservatum ecclesiasticum* should be settled once for all by a general imperial rescript. The moment naturally seemed propitious for redressing those long-standing and bitter grievances, the occupation by Protestant administrators of bishoprics and abbeys held immediately of the Empire, and the confiscation of smaller conventual estates by Protestant, especially Calvinist, governments. The Elector of Saxony at once showed signs of alarm, and it was some time before the Emperor himself was gained over to the scheme. But it opened too seductive a prospect for rewarding his faithful servants, and for endowing the cadets of his house, such as his son Leopold William, for whom were destined the great North German sees of Bremen, Verden, Minden, Halberstadt, and Magdeburg. Neither, however, was the religious side of the question lost sight of; and the Emperor's confessor, Lammermann, and the Papal nuncio, Caraffa, looked forward not only to the restoration of wealth to the Church, but also to the salvation of hundreds of thousands of souls. In many Catholic eyes the recovery of the whole of Germany was a mere question of time, and Ferdinand II.'s own mind was peculiarly open to such ideas. Thus the Edict of Restitution promulgated by him (March 1629) was so radical in its provisions as to render every archbishopric, bishopric, or ecclesiastical foundation whatever immediate to the Empire, that had not been in Protestant hands before 1552, liable to being forcibly brought back into the Roman commmunion; while the retrospective validity of the *reservatum ecclesiasticum* for the period 1517–1552 was left a dangerously open question. Implicitly, the exercise in the Empire of any Confession by the side of the Roman except that of Augsburg was prohibited; explicitly, the expulsion of Protestant inhabitants from the territories of Catholic estates was approved. This latter proceeding, though at the time of the religious Peace of Augsburg the attempt had been expressly made to guard against it, had been persistently resorted to by Catholic, especially spiritual, princes.

The execution of the edict spread terror far and near among the Protestant Estates, both those which had taken part in the Danish war and those which, like Saxony, had loyally abstained from opposing the Emperor in arms. Material interests, and religious and educational likewise, to a very considerable extent, were threatened by its incidence. In the imperial cities of Elsass, in the diocese of Augsburg, in the feudal network of the Franconian circle, the edict was carried out with relentless rigour; and it was enforced in those parts of the Empire which, like the Lower Saxon circle, were still under the control of the Liguistic or imperial forces, while passive and at times active resistance was opposed to it in Würtemberg, Hesse-Cassel, and the neighbouring districts, and elsewhere. By the autumn of 1631 there had been recovered for the Church of Rome two archbishoprics, Bremen and Magdeburg, after fire and sword had overthrown this 'Chancery of God,' five bishoprics, two immediate abbeys, and nearly 150 churches and convents, with about 200 parsonages in villages and towns hitherto Protestant, and a great increase of these numbers was in near prospect. From the nature of the case, a large proportion of the recoveries fell to the older and less active orders, the Benedictines and the Cistercians; but the Jesuits were vigilant, and would probably in the end have been the

*Results of its execution.*

chief gainers. On the other hand, great indignation was excited among the members of the League by the application of so many of the gains to the purposes of the Habsburg dynasty, and by the unscrupulous action of the imperial general, Wallenstein. These differences, which led to the dismissal of Wallenstein (June 1630), did not interfere with the operation of the edict, but they encouraged John George of Saxony to manœuvre against it, and at the Frankfort Convention (autumn 1631) to demand its revocation. Had this demand, or that of Bavaria for a postponement of execution for forty years, been granted, the revolt of Saxony and the Estates following her lead might conceivably even now have been averted. As it was, after the fruits of the alliance between Saxony and Gustavus Adolphus had been swiftly secured by his great victory at Breitenfeld (September 17, 1631), the Edict of Restitution become a dead letter. About half the operations taken in hand under its provisions had been actually carried out before the close of the year 1631. The collapse of the victorious reaction marked by the edict was due to the sword of Gustavus Adolphus, but it was prepared in no small measure by the fears and jealousies excited by the edict itself.

The year notable for the issue of the Edict of Restitution is also marked by the last Huguenot rising in France. When its leader, Rohan, accepted the agreement known as the Peace of Alais, a chapter closed in the history of France and of French Protestantism. The latter ceased to be an *imperium in imperio*, and Richelieu began to feel his hands free for a national policy of opposition to the

*Franco and Gustavus Adolphus.*

House of Habsburg, and in the first instance to Spain. Skilfully availing himself of Italian feeling and of Pope Urban VIII.'s growing opposition to the Habsburg policy, he intervened with a high hand in the question of the Mantuan succession (1630-31), effected secret understandings with Savoy and Bavaria, and concluded an agreement with Gustavus Adolphus, of which he of course intended to keep the development in his own hands. During the wonderful years 1631 and 1632 the European problem seemed at last to have found its master in the great Swedish king. But neither the deeds nor the plans of Gustavus Adolphus belong to the subject of this sketch. After his death (November 16, 1632), Richelieu preceived in the new condition of things the real opportunity of France; and by entering upon the deliberate execution of his great political plan, cut off all prospect of a revival under any conditions of the Catholic Reaction in the Empire. The Convention of Heilbronn (1633) kept alive the Protestant alliance, and had Wallenstein, aggrieved and ambitious, been actually tempted into an alliance with the foes of the Emperor, it might have proved possible to detach Bohemia and its dependencies under a national king from the Habsburg rule, and they might have recovered their religious liberties in due sequence. But this was not to be. Wallenstein's assassination (February 1634), though it removed a serious obstacle to the complete reunion of the interests of the two branches of the House of Habsburg, helped to secure to France the decisive voice in the affairs of Europe; and France neither would nor could assent to any pacific settlement, which, by restor-

*French intervention after the death of Gustavus Adolphus.*

ing to the Catholic reaction the advantages formerly gained by it, should have crowned the Habsburg policy with success. Thus, though the great victory of Nördlingen (September 1634) made the Emperor master of the whole of the south-west, it only led to the Treaty of Paris, which threw into the arms of France the German members of the League of Heilbronn (November), unwillingly followed by Sweden. On the other hand, the Protestant princes of the northern part of the Empire, headed by the Elector of Saxony, soon concluded with the Emperor the Peace of Prague (May 1635). This treaty left in the hands of the Protestants princes included in it all their mediate acquisitions, and all the immediate territories obtained by them before 1627 —in other words, the greater part of the Northern bishoprics—and therefore, in substance, undid the Edict of Restitution. No mention was, however, made either of the Bohemian liberties or of a possible restoration of Protestant rights in the hereditary dominions of the House of Austria; and the benefits of this treaty, as of the religious peace concluded eighty years before, were not extended to the Calvinists. This compromise with the Lutheran interest, which the Edict of Restitution had so unwisely offended, was strongly opposed by Urban VIII. and the Jesuit influence at Vienna, but supported by F. Quiroga and other leading Capuchins.

*The Peace of Prague.*

During the weary and awful years which remained of the Great War (1635–48), the religious character of the struggle was nearly altogether lost. In the real forefront of the

*The war loses its character as a religious struggle.*

fight stood on opposite sides the two great Catholic powers France and Spain, and the attitude of the head of the Church contributed to the confusion of accustomed conceptions. While Richelieu was unfolding his designs for the overthrow of the Habsburg ascendancy, Urban VIII. was quarrelling with Cardinal Borgia, who represented Spanish interests at the Vatican; and the more fiery adherents of Spain bethought themselves of setting the cumbrous machinery of a General Council to work against the Pope. Gradually, however, his eyes were opened to the futility of his devices for counterbalancing the power of the House of Habsburg without damaging the Catholic cause; and before long he once more paid subsidies to the Emperor. The election of his successor, Innocent X. (Pamfili, 1644–55), was accounted a victory for Spain; but he was a pontiff of slight personal significance, and his support proved of very secondary value to the House of Habsburg in the last phases of the struggle. The task of Ferdinand III. (1637–58) was simply to preserve as far as possible the integrity of his dynastic inheritance, and to save what he could save of the remnants of the imperial authority. He succeeded better in the attempt than his father might have done, being readier to temper zeal with discretion, and though blameless in his life, standing less under ecclesiastical control.

*Pope Innocent X.*

*Ferdinand III.*

The contest had not yet been fought out to its final issue when Richelieu died (December 1642). But the mighty impulse which he had given to the policy of France must have survived, even had his dying recommendation of Mazarin as his

*Mazarin.*

successor failed to be respected by Lewis XIII. Thus, though after the young king's death (May 1643) the regency of France was in the hands of a princess of Spanish birth (Anne of Austria), the policy of France pursued its consistent course, encouraged by the great victories of Condé and Turenne, the successes of the Swedes, and the stir created on the eastern frontier by Prince George Rákóczy of Transylvania.

Peace had become an absolute necessity for the House of Austria, as well as for Bavaria, who sought by doubtful manœuvres to hasten its conclusion, and for the other parts of the Empire, which foreign invasion and occupation had sucked dry of their very life's blood. Spain had been likewise unfortunate in her struggle against France, with whose ally, the United Provinces, Philip IV. concluded peace in January 1648.

The Peace of Westphalia, which followed in the autumn of the same year, did not put an end to the persecutions whereby the Catholic powers continued from time to time to assert their right of counter-reformation; the Bohemian Protestants suffered anew in 1651 and 1652, and the Vaudois in 1655. Neither, of course, did it arrest the propaganda of private conversion, which was peculiarly active among the princely houses of the Empire and in other quarters in the latter half of the seventeenth century, nor allay the spirit of religious animosity between the Confessions. On the other hand, it put an end to the long-sustained endeavour, begun under Philip II., renewed under Ferdinand II., but never resumed after him, to re-establish the dominion of the Church of Rome over the whole of Western

*Religious aspects of the Peace of Westphalia.*

and Central Europe. So far as the Empire was concerned, the progress of Catholicism was very definitely arrested at the point which it had reached on January 1, 1624, the date now fixed as regulating the tenure of ecclesiastical lands. Bohemia and those hereditary territories of the House of Austria which had more or less fallen away from the faith were now secured to Rome. In Hungary, however, as has been seen, Protestantism had obtained a measure of concession. Bavaria retained the Upper Palatinate as the reward of her efforts, but the Lower was restored to the Protestant Palatine line. The other territorial changes in the Empire, including the cessions made for the "satisfaction" of the Swedish and French crowns, effected no violent alteration in the balance of the Confessions; but the Protestants, Calvinists as well as Lutherans, had gained the full acknowledgment of the right of every territorial sovereign to determine the established religion of his lands, the toleration of private worship being—except in the hereditary dominions of the House of Austria—secured to all three forms of faith alike. At the diet religious questions were henceforth to be settled by arrangement, or not at all; and the securities thus obtained derived additional strength from the recognition of the right of the princes of the Empire to form alliances as territorial sovereigns with other powers. More dubious was the advantage accruing from the *locus standi* for intervention in the affairs of the Empire granted to France and Sweden.

*Catholic and Protestant gains.*

Richelieu's services to Protestantism were not limited to the changes wrought in the religious condition of the Empire. His policy had indirectly contributed to the success of the English Revolution, and Mazarin's alliance with the Protectorate (1655) was in full accordance with the system continued by him. In unhappy Ireland, the great insurrection of 1641 had served as a pretext to victorious Puritanism for establishing an abnormal and unnatural religious as well as proprietary ascendancy. It is said that in France itself Richelieu at different times hoped to restore religious unity to the nation by conference, by concessions, even by corruption; but on such designs at least Rome and the Holy Office could place a sufficient veto. That he hereupon aimed at a schism in one or another form was denied by himself; but he constantly combated the pretensions of the clergy to independence as towards the state, and in the struggle which ensued the Jesuits allowed themselves to be played off by him against the Sorbonne. These difficulties descended to his successor, notwithstanding the victories of France over Spain. In Spain itself, as in Italy and the Catholic cantons of Switzerland, Catholicism had maintained its position; but the intimate alliance between the two branches of the House of Habsburg was drawing to a close, and the day of Spain's greatness in Europe, which had made the Counter-Reformation possible, was vanishing for ever.

The Treaties of Westphalia furnished a durable guarantee of religious peace in Europe, because, notwithstanding much in them that was unnatural and much that was unjust, they on the whole corresponded in this, as in other respects, to the actually existing balance of

*End of the Counter-Reformation as a movement of religious re-conquest.*

opinions and sentiments in Europe. The Papal protest against the peace remained unheeded, and this not merely because canon law makes it impossible for the authority of the Pope to dissolve a public treaty between Catholics and non-Catholics, but also because the religious conditions of the peace agreed with the necessities of the case as generally recognised. In other words, the endeavour of the Counter-Reformation to dictate a revision of the religious map of Europe was by common consent allowed to have come to an end; nor was it within the power of any pope, emperor, or king to revive this attempt. Yet in a less specific sense the Counter-Reformation maintained its continuity in much of the enthusiasm and energy perceptible in the religious life of Western and Central Europe during subsequent generations. Nor can the movement ever wholly come to an end so long as the Church of Rome retains the character formed for her by the course of her history as well as by the principles of her existence.

# INDEX.

AACHEN, the religious conflict at, 144.
Acquaviva (Jesuit general), 158; his alleged condemnation of Mariana's teaching, 161.
*Admonet nos* (bull), 107.
Adrian VI. (Pope), the earlier career of, 7; significance of his election to the Papacy, 8; his relations with Charles V., *ib.*; demands urged on, by the Sacred College, 9; the attempt of, at a counter-reformation, 10 *seq.*; his failure and death, 13; Inquisitor-General, 48.
Ægidius of Viterbo, 9.
Alais, Peace of, 189.
Albert, Archduke, 170.
Albert V. of Bavaria, 44, 136, 140.
Albert of Prussia, 133.
Alexander. *See* PARMA.
Allen, Cardinal, 122.
Altemps. *See* HOHENEMS.
*Alumbrados*, the, 50.
Alva, Duke of, concludes peace with Paul IV., 76, 112; in the Netherlands, 119.
Amboise, the Conspiracy of, 82; the Convention of, 112.
Anabaptism, a common term for Protestant heterodoxy, 134.
'Anabaptists' expelled from Upper Austria, 183.
Andreæ, Jacob, 130.
Anjou, Francis Duke of, 114.
Anne of Austria, Queen of France, 193.
Anne of Denmark, Queen of Scotland and England, a convert to Rome, 154, 179, 186.
Antwerp, the fall of, 121.
Arabella Stuart, 125.
Araoz (Jesuit), 41.
Armada, the Great, 111, 121, 125.
Augsburg, Cardinal Otto Truchsess, Bishop of, 142; diets at, 136, 142, 184; *Interim*, the, 44, 69 *seq.*; Religious Peace of, the, 73.
Augustus I. of Saxony, the *Formula Concordiæ* of, 133.
Austria, Jesuits in, 44; Protestantism prevails in, 136; the religious policy of Maximilian II. in, 140; the measures of Rudolf II. in, 144; the counter-reformation in, under Ferdinand II., 183.
Avilla, Juan de, 31.

BADEN, Catholicism restored in, 141.
Bamberg, 142.
Bannez (Dominican), 159.
Barnabites, the, 29.
Bassi, M. de, 26.
Báthory, Gabriel, 173.
Bavaria, Jesuits in, 44; the counter-reformation in, 140.
Bayonne, Conference of, 112.
Béarn, restoration of the Church estates in, 178.
Belgic provinces, the, lost to Protestantism, 121.
Bellarmine, Cardinal, 111, 135, 153; made cardinal, 158; his controversy with James I., 162, 164.
Berulle, P. de, 168.
Bethlen Gabor, Prince of Transylvania, 176, 180.
Bobadilla (Jesuit), 33, 44.
Bocskai, Stephen, 171.
Bohemia, Jesuits in, 45; advance of Protestantism in, 136; repressive measures of Rudolf II in, 144, 171; the Letter of Majesty signed in, 175; the counter-reformation in, under Ferdinand II., 18 *seq.*, 194.
Bohemian Brethren, the, 136, 144.
Bologna, the agreement of, 15; the Council removed to, from Trent, 68, 70.
Bona Sforza, Queen of Poland, 148.
Borgia, Cardinal, 192.
Borgia, Francis, St., 41, 184.
Borromean or Golden League, the, 147.
Borromeo, Cardinal, 80, 106; his *Collegium Helveticum* at Milan, 147, 167.
Bossuet, Bishop of Meaux, 130.
Bourbon, Cardinal of, 115; dies, 116, 154.
Breda, peace negotiations at, 120.
Breitenfeld, the battle of, 189.
Bremen, archbishopric of, 188.
Broussaet (Jesuit), 33.
Bruno, Giordano, 163.
Brussels capitulates to Parma, 121.
Bucer, Martin, 131.

# INDEX.

Buckingham, Duke of, 185.
Burlamacchi, Francesco, 142.

CAJETANO (de Vio), Cardinal, 12.
Calvin, 131.
Calvinism, the militant policy of, 157; conflicts of, with Saxony and Brandenburg, 172 *seq.*; dogmatic labours of, 179.
Camaldolites, the Reformed, 26.
Campeggi, Cardinal, 14.
Campion, Edmund (Jesuit), 124.
Canisius (Jesuit), in Austria, 44; at the Conference of Worms, 45; his *Summa Doctrinæ Christianæ*, *ib.*; in Poland, *ib.*; his *Catechisms*, 97, 137, 149.
Capuchins, the, 26 *seq.*
Caraffa, Carlo, Cardinal, 76.
Caraffa, Carlo (Nuncio), 183 *note*, 187.
Caraffa, Gian Pietro. *See* PAUL IV.
Cardinals, the College of, reformed, 106.
Carinthia, 136.
Carmelites, the Discalced, 104.
Carniola, 136.
Carranza, Archbishop of Toledo, 50, 63, 66, 102.
Carvajal, Cardinal, 9.
Catharine de' Medici, Queen of France, 82; her trimming policy, 83, 113.
Catharine, Queen of Sweden, 127.
Cervino, Cardinal, at Trent, 62.
Chambord, Alliance of, 72.
Chantal, Baroness de, 167.
Charles, Archduke of Styria, 144.
Charles V., Emperor, and Adrian VI., 8; loses his great opportunity of reformation, 15; adheres to the scheme of a General Council, 24; the relations of, with the Inquisition, 48 *seq.*; demands a General Council, 59; receives the Cardinal of Lorraine at Innsbruck, 91.
Charles I. of England, 185.
Charles IX. of Sweden, 127, 129.
Charles Emmanuel I. of Savoy, 111, 115; attempts to escalade Geneva, 163, 167.
Chastel, Jean, 155.
Chieregati, Francesco (Papal Legate), 13.
Christian I. of Anhalt, 157; the chief agent of the Palatinate policy of aggression, 173.
Christian III. of Denmark, 129 *seq.*
Christian IV. of Denmark, 184.
Christian I. of Saxony, 146.
Christian II. of Saxony, 146, 172.
Chytræus, David, 140.
Clement VII., Pope, the policy of, 14 *seq.*
Clement VIII., Pope, grants absolution to Henry IV., 155, 156; the religious policy of, 162.
Codure (Jesuit), 33.
Coimbra, the Jesuit College at, 42.
Coligny, Admiral, 113.
*Collegium Germanicum*, 40, 45.
*Collegium Romanum*, 40.
Cologne, Archbishop Gebhard II. of, attempts to Protestantise his electorate, 145; Ernest of Bavaria, Archbishop of, *ib.*; Peace congress at, 121.
Commendone, Bishop of Zante, 91, 138.
Condé, Louis I., Prince of, the death of, 112.

Condé, Henry I., Prince of, 115.
Condé, Louis II., Prince of, 196.
Conferences, religious, in Germany, 24 *seq.*
*Confessio Augustana*, 31.
*Confessio Tetrapolitana*, 31.
Congregation, the, of the Holy Office, 52; of the Index, 57; of the Council of Trent, 97.
*Concilium de emendandâ ecclesiâ*, 58.
Contarini, Cardinal, warns Clement VII., 16, 19; the first of Paul III.'s new cardinals, 22; the soul of the reform commission, 23; at Ratisbon, 25.
Council of Blood, the, in the Netherlands, 119.
Councils, the great, of the fifteenth century, and projects of reformation, 2.
Counter-reformation, the, attempted by Adrian VI., 10 *seq.*; the, in Bavaria, 140; in Baden, 141; in Fulda, *ib.*; in the Eichsfeld, 142; in the spiritual electorates and principalities, 16 *seq.*; progress of, under Rudolf II., 143 *seq.*; in Poland, 149 *seq.*; in Bohemia, 181 *seq.*; in Austria, 183; in the Palatinate, *ib.*; further hopes of, after the Danish war, 186; in what sense ended by the Peace of Westphalia, 196.
Cracow, Jesuit influence in the University of, 150 *seq.*
Crescentio, Cardinal, 72; dies, 73.
Crespy, the Peace of, 60.
Crypto-Calvinism in Saxony, 146.
Cruz, Juan de la, 104.
Cup, the concession of the, to the laity, 8.

DANISH war, the results of the, 184; the Catholic satisfaction at, 185.
*Dejados*, the, 50.
Delfins, J. (Papal Nuncio), 138.
Demetrius, the false, 166.
Denmark, Protestant intolerance in, 130
Desmond, the Earl of, the insurrection of, 126.
Diet, the, of the Empire, religious questions at, after the Peace of Westphalia, 194.
Dillingen, the University of, 142.
Dio, Juan di, 31.
Dominicans, the, and the Inquisition, 47; and the Index, 55; controversy of, with the Jesuits, 159.
Donauwörth, the counter-reformation at, 174.
Dorpat, the Jesuit College at, 150.
Dort, the Synod of, 179.
Douay, the English College at, 123.
Duplessis-Mornay, Philip, 166.

EASTERN Churches, the proposed reunion of, under Papal supremacy, 164.
Eichsfeld, the, 142.
Elizabeth of England, 77; and Paul IV., 78, 82; excommunicated, 107; hopes of the conversion of, 122 *seq.*; plots against, 124, 134.
England, the Marian reaction in, 76 *seq.*; the Catholic propaganda in, 122; Catholic efforts in, under James I., 153 *seq.*; 179.

# INDEX.

Erasmus, D., his idea of reformation, 6; and Adrian VI., 12.
Eric XIV. of Sweden, 127.
Ernest, Archduke, 170.
Ernest of Bavaria, Bishop of Münster, 142; Archbishop of Cologne, 145.
Essex, Earl of, 153.

FAENZA, Jesuits at, 40.
Ferdinand I., Emperor, 44; urges the assembling of a General Council in a German town, 81; his *Libellus de reformatione* at Trent, 83; appeals for a settlement to Pius IV., 91; his bargain with Pius IV., 92; the advance of Protestantism under, 135.
Ferdinand II., Emperor, his counter-reformation in Styria, 144, 170; chosen as future head of the House of Austria, 176, 178; his schemes and hopes, 186.
Ferdinand III., Emperor, the character of, 192.
Ferrara added to the Papal dominions, 163.
*Feuillants*, the, 167 *seq.*
Fischart, Johann, 147.
Flacius, Matthias, 133.
Flagellants, the, in France, 114.
Fleix, Peace of, 114.
Fontainebleau, Assembly of Notables at, 82.
*Formula Concordiæ*, the, 130, 133 *seq.*
France, the religious condition of, under Henry II., 81; under Francis II., 82; the religious wars of, 112 *seq.*; the close of the religious conflict in, 154; under Maria de' Medici, 168 *seq.*; under Richelieu, 185; under Louis XIII., 193.
François de Sales, St., 167.
Frankfort-on-Main, Convention of, 139.
Frederick II. of Denmark, 130.
Frederick IV., Elector Palatine, 132.
Frederick IV., Elector Palatine, 157, 172.
Frederick V., Elector Palatine, 154, 177, 179.
Fregoso, Cardinal, 22.
Fulda, Abbot Balthazar, of, 141; counter-reformation in, 141.
Funcke, J. F., 133.

GAETANO of Thiene, 28.
Gandamus, N., 44.
Gardie, Pontus de la, 128.
Gebhard II. See COLOGNE.
Gemblours, the battle of, 121.
Geneva and Savoy, 111, 147, 163.
Germany, the disunion of the Protestants in, 172; the attempts at union among the Protestants in, 173.
Ghent, the Pacification of, 120.
Ghiberti, Cardinal, 19, 22.
Giustiniani, P., 26.
Gondomar, Count, 179.
Gonzaga, Cardinal, 88; dies, 91.
Granada, Archbishop Guerrero, of, 86.
Granvelle, Cardinal, 24.
Gras, Louise de, 168.
Gregorian Calendar, the, 109.
Gregory XIII., Pope, 105; the government and policy of, 108 *seq.*, 127.

Gregory XIV., Pope, adheres to Spain and the League, 154.
Gregory XV., Pope, 183.
Grey Sisters, the, in France, 168.
Grisons, the, 169.
Guise, the House of, 81, 115.
Guise, Cardinal, assassinated, 115.
Guise, Francis, Duke of, 93.
Guise, Henry, Duke of, assassinated, 115.
Gunpowder Plot, the, 153.
Gustavus I. Vasa, 126.
Gustavus II. Adolphus, 184; the German victories of, 189; his relations with Richelieu, 190.

HABSBURG family compact, the, 71.
Hedwig, Princess, of Denmark, 179.
Heidelberg Catechism, the, 132.
Heilbronn, Convention of, 190.
Henry II. of France, 69, 72, 81.
Henry III. of France, the instability of, 114; in Poland, 149.
Henriquez (Jesuit), 158.
Henry IV. of France and Navarre, 113; a claimant to the French throne, 114; negotiates with Sixtus V., 116, 154; abjures Protestantism, 155; his religious policy on the throne, 156; his schemes against the House of Habsburg, *ib.*, 165; the Catholic revival in France under, 167 *seq.*; assassinated, 168, 176.
Hildesheim, 142.
Hoë von Hoënegg, 172.
Hohenems, Cardinal, 84.
Hosius, Cardinal, Legate at Trent, 84, 127, 138, 148.
Huguenots, the last insurrection of the, 189.
Hungary, the advance of Protestantism in, 140; repressive measures of Rudolf II. in, 144, 171; revolution in, *ib.*; Protestantism maintains itself in, throughout the Thirty Years' War, 180.

ILLESHAZI, Stephen, 171.
*Immensa æterna Dei* (bull), 110.
*In cœna Domini* (bull), 107, 184.
Index, the, in Spain, 55; earliest examples of the compilation of, by Papal authority, 56 *seq.*; in Spain, 102.
Ingolstadt, Jesuits at, 44, 141.
*Injunctum nobis* (bull), 35.
Innocent IX., Pope, 155.
Innocent X., Pope, 192.
Inquisition, the, the Spanish origin of, 47; the relations of, with the Popes in the period preceding the Reformation, *ib.*; under Ximenez, *ib.*; Adrian, 48; Manrique, *ib.*; Valdez, 49; Philip II. undertakes the protection of, *ib.*; powers conferred on by Paul IV., *ib.*, 79; crushes Protestantism out of Spain, *ib. seq.*; attempts to introduce, into the Netherlands, France, 50 *seq.*; and Naples, 52; effects of, in Italy, 54 *seq.*; maintains its authority in Spain under Philip III., 178.
Ireland, early Jesuit mission to, 39; insurrections in, and Spanish attempts upon, 126, 153; Protestant ascendancy established in, 195.

Italy, spiritual movements in, during the earlier part of the sixteenth century, 18; moral and intellectual effects of the counter-reformation on, 116 seq.

JAMES I. of England, Catholic expectations of, 153; plots against, ib.; controversy of, with Bellarmine, ib., 162; allied with the Protestant Union, 177.
James III. of Baden-Hochberg, a convert to Catholicism, 146.
January Edict, the, 83.
Jarnac, battle of, 112.
Jesuits. See JESUS, THE COMPANY OF.
Jesus, the Company or Order of, 31 seq.; indigenous to Spain, 32; its earliest members, 33; their arrival at Rome, 34; confirmed by Paul III., 35; its *Constitutions*, ib.; *Declarations*, 36; so-called *Secret Institutions*, ib.; the cardinal points in its system, ib. seq.; its early progress in Italy, 39 seq.; in Spain, 40 seq.; in Portugal, 41 seq.; in France, 42 seq.; in the Netherlands, 43; in Germany, ib. seq.; in Poland, 45; its distant missions, 46; the condition of, at the time of the death of its founder, ib.; fully established at Rome, 52, 109; influx of members of, into France, 115; influence of, in Italy, 117; missionary propaganda of, in England, 117; the mission of, in England (1580), 123 seq.; colleges of, in Flanders, &c., 125; members of, in Sweden, 128; Bavaria, 140; the spiritual territories, 141; Switzerland, 147; Poland, 149, 153; banished from France, 155; readmitted thither, 156; internal dissensions in, 157 seq.; the Molinist controversy in, 160; teachings on tyrannicide in, 160 seq.; missions of, into remote parts, 163; recalled into France, 167; activity of, in the Bohemian counter-reformation, 182; and the Edict of Restitution, 188.
Jews, the, persecuted by Paul IV., 79.
Joachim Frederick of Brandenburg, 173.
John, Don, of Austria, 120.
John III. of Sweden, attempts a counter-reformation, 127; his *Red Book*, 128.
John Casimir, Count Palatine, 132, 146.
John George I. of Saxony, 172, 178, 187.
John Sigismund of Brandenburg, 173.
Joyeuse, Cardinal, 165.
Juliers succession, the question of the, 175 seq.
Jungbunzlau, 171.
Justification, decree on, at the Council of Trent, 67.

KHLESL, Bishop of Vienna, 174.
Kroll, Chancellor, 146.

LAINEZ (Jesuit general), 33, 37; succeeds Loyola as general, 46; at Trent, 86, 93.
Lammermann (confessor of Ferdinand II.), 187.
Landshut, the Jesuit College at, 141.
Lasco, John a, 130, 148.
Lateran Council, the fifth, 3, 5.
Lazarists, the, 168.
League, the Catholic, in Germany, founded, 175.

League, the Holy, in France, 114.
Le Fèvre (Jesuit), 33, 43; in Germany, ib.
Le Jay (Jesuit), 33, 37, 44.
Lennox, Earl of (Esmé Stuart), 125.
Leo X., Pope, and the religious movement, 18.
Leo XI., Pope, 103.
Leon, Luis de, 102.
Leopold, William, Archduke, 176; an ecclesiastical arch-pluralist, 187.
Lepanto, the battle of, 108.
Lerma, Count, 178.
Letter of Majesty, the, granted, 175; violated, 176.
*Licet ab initio* (bull), 52.
Liechtenstein, Prince Charles of, 181.
Lippomano, A. (Papal Legate), 72.
Livonia, the Catholic reaction in, 150.
Lodovisio, Cardinal, 183.
Lope de Vega, 50.
Lorraine, the Cardinal of, 42, 51, 81; urges reforms at Trent, 90; visits Charles V. at Innsbruck, 91; gained over by Pius IV., 93, 97, 99.
Los Angeles, Juan of, 31.
Louis XIII. of France, 193.
Louvain, the Jesuits at, 43; the Index of the University of, 56.
Loyola, Ignatius, St., 31 seq.; his *Spiritual Exercises*, 36; the proposal to canonise, 162; canonised, 184.
Lucca, the Inquisition at, 54; the meeting at, between Charles V. and Paul III., 59.
Lucerne, 169.
Lübeck, Peace of, 186.
Luna, Count, 95.
Luther and the Papacy, 6, 131; effects of his death, 132.
Lutheranism, the rigidity of, 131.
Luxemburg, Duke of, at Rome, 116.

MADRE de Dios, Jerome Gratian de la, 104.
Madruccio, Cardinal, 61, 66.
Maestricht, the sack of, 121.
Magdeburg, 188.
Malaspina (Papal Legate), 129, 166.
Manrique (Inquisitor-General), 48, 159.
Mantuan succession, the, 185, 190.
Marcellus II., Pope, 74.
Margaret. See PARMA.
Maria de' Medici, Queen of France, 167; her policy as regent, 168 seq.
Mariana (Jesuit), 158; his *De rege et regis institutione*, 160 seq.
Mary I. of England, the religious reaction under, 76 seq.
Mary, Queen of Scots, and the Council of Trent, 93, 120; a fugitive in England, 123.
Matthias, Emperor, as Archduke, 170; intrigues against Rudolf II., 173; acquires the greater part of his dominions, 174; succeeds as Emperor, 176; his helplessness, 177.
Maurice of Saxony, 71, 73.
Maximilian I. of Bavaria, 172, 176.
Maximilian II., Emperor, 92, 107; his inclination towards Protestantism, 137; restrained from renouncing Catholicism, 138; the tolerant character and policy of, 139 seq.

Mayenne, Duke of, 154.
Melanchthon, Philip, 133.
Mendoza, Count, 59, 64.
Michna, Count Paul, 181.
Minims, the, 26.
Missions of the Church of Rome into remote parts, 163.
Mocenigo, Doge, 114.
Molina (Jesuit), 159.
Monçon, Peace of, 185.
Monsieur, Peace of, 114.
Moors, the, expelled from Spain, 178.
Moravia, 183.
Morone, Cardinal, 59, 78; Legate at Trent, 91.
Mühlhausen, 147, 186.
Münster, the counter-reformation in, 142; John of Hoya and Ernest of Bavaria, Bishops of, ib.
Munich, Jesuit college at, 141.

NANTES, Edict of, 156.
Nasus (Franciscan), 147.
Naumburg, Convention of, 82.
Navagero, Cardinal (Papal Legate), 92.
Netherlands, the revolt of the, largely due to religious causes, 118; the progress of, 119; final adjustment of the struggle in the, 121.
Nîmes, Edict of, 185.
Nördlingen, battle of, 191.
Northern Rebellion, the, in England, 123.
Nürnberg, Diet of (1523), 13.

OCHINO, Bernardino, 22, 27, 40, 53.
Olivarez, Count, 111, 186.
Oratory, the, of Divine Love at Rome, 19: the precedent of, followed at Vicenza and elsewhere, ib.; the Congregation of the, at Rome, 30.
Orders, new monastic, from the latter part of the fifteenth century onward, 26 seq.
Osiander, Lucas, 133.

PACHECO, Cardinal, 63, 66, 79.
Paderborn, 142, Bishop Theodore of Fürstenberg of, 172.
Padua and the religious revival, 20, 54.
Palatinate, the, the Calvinist era in, 132 seq.; the aggressive policy of, 173 seq.; bestowed upon Max of Bavaria, 183; the Upper, retained by Bavaria, 194.
Paris, the Parliament of, and the Inquisition, 51; Treaty of (1634), 191.
Parma, Alexander of, 121; dies, 122, 155.
Parma, Margaret of, 43, 119.
Parsons, Robert (Jesuit), 124.
Pasquier-Brouet (Jesuit), 39.
*Pastoralis officii cura* (bull), 35.
Paul III., Pope, motives of the policy of, 17; creates new cardinals, 22; appoints a commission on Church reform, 33; confirms the Order of Jesus, 35; summons a General Council to Mantua, 59; to Vicenza and to Trent, ib.; the motives of, in assembling the Council, ib.; the rupture of, with Charles V., 68; dies, 70.
Paul IV. (Pope), supports the ecclesiastical policy of Adrian VI., 12, 19; the earlier experiences of, 20; a founder of the Theatines, 28; confers new powers on the Inquisition, 49, 52; significance of the election to the Papacy of, 74; his hatred of Spain and the Emperor, 75; failure of his anti-Spanish policy, 76; the counter-reformation of, 79; dies, 80, 138.
Paul V., Pope, 162; the religious revival under, 163; his quarrel with Venice, 164 seq. 178.
Paulines, the, 29.
Pázmány, Cardinal, 180.
Peter Martyr (Vermigli), 53.
Peter of Alcantara, St., 30, 104.
Phauser, Sebastian, 137.
Philip of Baden-Hochberg, 141.
Philip II. of Spain, 42; his policy at Trent, 83, 88; his religious policy, 101; his relations with the Inquisition, 102; with Sixtus V., 111; intervenes in the French religious conflict, 112, 115; failure of his schemes, 152, 156.
Philip III. of Spain, 176; the religious and political ideas of, 178.
Philip IV. of Spain, 193.
Philip of Neri, St., 29 seq., 108.
Pighino, Alberti (Legate), 72.
Pisa, the so-called Council of, 4.
Pistorius, Johann (Catholic divine), 146.
Pius IV., Pope, the character and government of, 80; his procedure at Trent, 91 seq.
Pius V., Pope, 53; the religious policy of, 107; Poissy, Colloquy of, 86.
Poland, the Reformation in, 148; restoration of Catholic ascendancy in, 166 seq.
Pole, Cardinal, at Padua, 21; at Viterbo, 44; at Trent, 59; proposed for the Papacy, 70; in England, 77; dies, 78.
Popes, the, of the century before the Reformation, 3.
Possevin (Jesuit), 128.
Postel (Jesuit), 42.
*Postynam verus ille* (bull), 110.
Prague, the battle of, 181; Peace of, 191; Archbishop Ernest von Harrach of, 181.
Protestantism penetrates into Italy, 21, 24; the progress of, in Germany and the neighbouring countries, 47; crushed out of Spain by the Inquisition, 49 seq.; and out of Italy, 53 seq.; the variations of, 130; disunion between the chief divisions of, 132; attempts at a dogmatic union of, 133 seq.; heterodox movements in, 134; advance of, in the empire under Ferdinand I., 135 seq.; and Maximilian II., 140; in Poland, 148 seq.; repulsed, 151; attempts at a union of, in Germany, 173; the prospects of, before the death of Henry IV. of France, 176; disunion in, before the outbreak of the Thirty Years' War, 179 seq.
Puteo, Cardinal, 84.

QUIROGA (Capuchin), 191.

RÁKÓCZY, George, Prince of Transylvania, 180, 193.
Raleigh, Sir Walter, 179.

Ratisbon, religious conference at (1541), 25.
Ratisbon, François, *Interim,* the, 25.
Ravaillac, 168.
Reformation in the Church of Rome, attempts at, before and in the Conciliar period, 1; the general desire for, in the fifteenth century, 3; the idea of a, by Papal authority, abandoned, 6.
Reformation, the Protestant. *See* PROTESTANTISM.
*Regimini* (bull), 35.
*Reichskammergericht,* the, treatment of Protestant grievances by, 172.
Renée of Ferrara, 54.
*Reservatum ecclesiasticum,* the, 137, 186 *seq.*
Residence, decree on, at Trent, proposed, 67; resumed, 87 *seq.*
Restitution, the Edict of, 186 *seq.*; results of its execution, 188 *seq.*; becomes a dead letter, 189; undone by the Peace of Prague, 191.
Rheims, English College transferred to, 123.
Richelieu, Cardinal, at the head of affairs in France, 185; the cautious foreign policy of, *ib.*; unfolds his policy against Habsburg, 189 *seq.*; dies, 192; his services to Protestantism, 194 *seq.*
Richer, Edmond, 168.
Ridolfi plot, the, 123.
Riga, 150.
Rochelle, the fall of, 185.
Rodriguez (Jesuit), 33.
Rohan, Prince of, 189.
Rome, the sack of, 15; its significance in the history of the Church of, and of the Renascence, 16, 19; the counter-reformation at, 106; the English College at, 123.
Romorantin, the Edict of, 51.
Rudolf II., Emperor, the training and character of, 143; the Catholic reaction under, 169 *seq.*; the brothers and sisters of, 170; the mania and impotence of, 173; deprived of most of his dominions by Matthias, 174.
Ruthven, the Raid of, 125.

SADOLETT, Cardinal, 19, 22.
Salmeron (Jesuit), 33, 39, 86.
Salzburg, Protestantism in, 136; religious reaction in, under Archbishop Wolf Dietrich von Raitenau, *ib.*
St. Bartholomew, Massacre of, 108; the responsibility of the, 113.
St. Germain, Peace of, 113.
St. Quintin, battle of, 76.
Sanchez, Francisco de, 102.
Sanders, Nicolas, 126.
Sarpi (Fra Paolo), the mouthpiece of Venice in her quarrel with Paul V. and the Jesuits, 165.
Sebastian of Portugal, 42, 83.
Ségur, Count, in Germany, 134.
Seripando, Cardinal, 84; dies, 91.
Servetus, Michael, 107.
Sigismund II. Augustus of Poland, 99, 148.
Sigismund III. of Sweden and Poland, 129; fully restores Catholicism in Poland, 150 *seq.*, 166, 179.

Silesia, 183.
Silvanus executed, 133.
Simonetta, Cardinal, 84.
Sixtus V., Pope, the earlier career of, 109; the religious and foreign policy of, 110 *seq.*; becomes favourable to the independence of France, 115; by keeping out of an alliance with Philip II. preserves France from Spain, 116, 146.
Smalcaldic War, the, outbreak of, 66.
Smerwick, massacre of, 128.
Socinianism, the rise of, 135.
Soderini, Cardinal, 12.
Somascines, the, 29.
Sorbonne, the, and the Jesuits, 42, 60.
Soto, Dominico de, 63.
Spain and the counter-reformation, 101; the intellectual condition of, under Philip II., 103; under Philip III., 178; after the Thirty Years' War, 195.
Spanish mysticism, early efforts of, 30 *seq.*; the spiritual influence of, 103.
Spanish theatre, the, under Philip II., 103; under Philip III., 178.
Spanish universities, the, under Philip II. and Philip III., 103.
Stephen Bathory (of Poland), 111, 149 *seq.*
Stralsund, 186.
Strasburg, 135; schism in the chapter at, 145.
Styria, advance of Protestantism in, 136; the religious visitation of, under Archduke Charles, 144; Archduke Ferdinand's counter-reformation in, 170.
Sweden, counter-reformation attempted in, 126 *seq.*
Switzerland, Catholic revival in, 169.

TASSO, Torquato, 116.
Teresa, St., 104 *seq.*; her *Interior Castle,* 105.
Territorial principle, the, in religion, 132.
Theatines, the, 28.
Thirty Years' War, the, Catholic and Protestant prospects of success in, 177, *seq.*; the general progress of, 180; the latter years of, 191 *seq.*
Toulouse, League of, 112.
Transylvania, the Unitarians of, 135, 171.
Trent, the Council of, first summoned by Paul III., 59; dispersed, *ib.*; summoned afresh, 60; circumstances of the assembling of, 61; the legates presiding over, 62; composition of, *ib. seq.*; order of business at, 64; work accomplished in the first eight sessions of, *ib. seq.*; conflicts between the Imperial and Papal parties at, *ib.*; decrees passed at, 68; removed to Bologna, *ib.*; reopens at Trent, 72; the second series of the sessions of, *ib. seq.*; Protestant ambassadors at, *ib.*; again suspended, 73; reassembled by Pius IV., 82; reopens, 83; the new presiding legates at, 84; question as to the continuity of, 85; question as to the legates' initiative at, *ib.*; composition of, in its concluding period, 86; discusses the questions of residence and of the concession of the Cup to the laity, 88 *seq.*; the French "libel" presented at, 90; the

# INDEX. 203

new legates at, 91; the policy of Pius IV. prevails at, *ib. seq.*; business of, wound up, 94; closing of, 95 *seq.*; reception of the decrees of, in the several States of Europe, 97 *seq.*; the results of, summarised, 100.
Treves, counter-reformation at, 142.
Turenne, Marshal, 193.
Tyrannicide, Jesuit teachings on, 160 *seq.*
Tyrone, Earl of, the insurrection of (1602), 126.

*Unam sanctam* (bull), 5.
Union, the Protestant, 157; its relations with Henry IV., 168; concluded at Ahausen, 175; the foreign alliances of, 176, 177.
United Provinces, the, allied with the Protestant Union, 177; conclude peace with Spain, 193.
Upsala, religious agreement at, 129.
Urban VII., Pope, 154.
Urban VIII., Pope, the anti-Habsburg policy of, 184, 186, 191 *seq.*
Ursulines, the, 30.
Utrecht, Union of, 121.

VALDEZ, Fernando (Inquisitor-General), 49.
Valdez, Juan, 22.
Valtelline, the, Spanish occupation of, 169; Richelieu intervenes in, 185.
Venegaz, Alejo, 31.
Venice, and the religious revival, 19 ; Protestant sympathies surviving at, 54; the quarrel of, with Paul V., 164 *seq.*
Ventimiglio, Bishop Visconti of, 84.
Vervins, Peace of, 148.
Villanueva (Jesuit), 41.
Vincent de Paula, St., 168.
Visitantines, the, 167.

WALDENSES, the, 55.
Wallenstein (Duke of Friedland), 186; dismissed, 189; assassinated, 190.
Westphalia, Peace of, its effects upon the counter-reformation, 193; Catholic and Protestant gains in, 194; a durable guarantee of religious peace, 195 *seq.*; Papal protest against, 196.
William IV. of Bavaria, 44, 140.
William I. of Juliers-Cleves-Berg, 140 *seq.*
William I. of Orange, 120.
Wilna, the University of, 150.
*Wittenberg Concordia*, the, 131.
Worms *gravamina*, the, 4; the religious discussion at, 136, 142.
Würtemberg, stability of Protestantism in, 141.
Würzburg, Julius Echter, Bishop of, 142; the University of, *ib.*

XAVIER, Francis, St., 33, 41, 46.
Ximenez, Cardinal, 4, 47.

ZAMOYSKI, J. S., 151.
Zapata (Jesuit), 39.

---

PRINTED BY BALLANTYNE, HANSON AND CO.
EDINBURGH AND LONDON

www.ingramcontent.com/pod-product-compliance
Lightning Source LLC
Chambersburg PA
CBHW020828230426
43666CB00007B/1139